D0030770

Elisabeth Kübler-Ross is the author of

Working It Through

An Elisabeth Kübler-Ross Workshop on Life, Death and Transition

text by ELISABETH KÜBLER-ROSS, M.D.

photographs by MAL WARSHAW

A TOUCHSTONE BOOK
Published by Simon & Schuster

TOUCHSTONE
Rockefeller Center
1230 Avenue of the Americas
New York, NY 10020

First Touchstone Edition 1997

TOUCHSTONE and colophon are registered trademarks
of Simon & Schuster Inc.

Manufactured in the United States of America

10   9   8   7   6   5   4   3   2   1

The Library of Congress has cataloged a previous edition as
follows:
    Working it through.
    Reprint. Originally published: New York : Macmillan, 1982.
    Includes index.
    1. Death — Social aspects.   2. Death — Religious
aspects.   I. Title.
[HQ1073.K8   1987]   306'.9   86-28412
ISBN 0-684-83942-3

To David. And the hundreds of Davids and Lindas and Bettys everywhere, who have truly given us a beautiful gift, and who have been our teachers.

Contents

Foreword by Elisabeth Kübler-Ross

In 1970, HAVING WORKED FOR many years with terminally ill patients confined to hospitals, I realized that I could help more people more effectively by meeting with them in groups on a day-to-day basis, outside an institutional environment. Thus we began the first of hundreds of our Workshops in Life, Death, and Transition, for those whose lives have been touched by death—be they terminally ill, the bereaved, doctors, nurses, social workers, clergy, or others involved with the dying. For periods of five days, the groups meet together morning, noon, and evening and share all their meals, so patients can describe their experiences to each other and learn to vent their feelings of fear, anger, grief, and above all, love. That is the subject of *Working It Through*.

Since 1970 we have established workshops in Europe, and as far away as Australia and New Zealand. Thousands of participants from every kind of background—racial, religious, ethnic, and economic—and of every age, from 11 to 104, have shared their innermost thoughts with us on death and dying.

But the nature of our workshops has also expanded. Special workshops have been set up for children and teens, who may be the victims of incest, abuse, or broken homes, and for women who have suffered such trauma as well.

Of extreme importance now are our separate sessions for AIDS patients, their families, friends, and health-care professionals who work with them. These will continue to be of the utmost importance until a cure for that deadly illness is found.

In addition, we have established a scholarship fund for those who are unable to afford our workshop fees. Much of that income comes from scarves I knit while traveling from place to place. We auction these at the end of each workshop and offer them in raffles. Each scarf is designed to pay for at least one patient, who usually wears that scarf during his or her final days, passing it on to another in need, thereby creating a link between present and future.

While some of our participants are anxious at first about sharing their thoughts in a group situation, many are able to overcome their inhibitions after hearing the stories of others. I always say that you have to be either a saint or a rock of Gibraltar not to be moved by the stories we hear, but there are still those who hesitate to participate in public. For that purpose we have set up sessions on a one-to-one basis—what I call our "backroom work." This slowly but surely helps our participants come out into the open and become part of our groups, helping them also overcome their suffering, and in the process, attain understanding.

Pain and anguish, tears and rage, love and forgiveness, these are the emotions that can be felt through the words of our participants, and they can be seen on their faces, as Mal Warshaw's photographs—silent witnesses to the dramas we hear day after day, week after week—attest. They also bear witness to the human strength and endurance, to faith and the ability to survive and transcend the most difficult trials in life.

I hope that this new edition of *Working It Through* will be an inspiration for all of us to reexamine our lives, to ask ourselves, if we only had a short time in which to live, to whom we own thanks, to whom we should make amends. For whom do we feel anger or guilt, and for whom love, perhaps inadequately expressed? And I hope it will help us all reach a physical, emotional, intellectual, and spiritual harmony so we can learn to live truly in the here and now, free to enjoy life, free, too, to look back with satisfaction at the end of our journey. For once we can learn to accept ourselves, to love and forgive ourselves, then we can learn to do so with others. The end result is an inner peace, a vital prerequisite for peace in the world.

Preface by Mal Warshaw

ON A SUBFREEZING MORNING IN January a few years ago I made a trip from my home in New York City to the suburbs of Chicago with a few photographs under my arm to meet Elisabeth Kübler-Ross. The losses I had experienced in my own life had led me to begin photographing a terminal cancer patient, and Elisabeth had agreed to look at the pictures. That meeting had a profound influence on my life and marked the beginning of a continuing friendship and collaboration resulting in this, our second book together.

This book illuminates the Elisabeth Kübler-Ross "Life, Death, and Transition Workshops" that are held periodically in various parts of the country.

I believe that photography has a special role to play in a book that sets out to document the workshops and to deal with the intimate, intense feelings that are a part of those experiences.

Feelings take place in time—often a short space of time. A photograph freezes a fraction of a second in time, in all its intricate detail. It allows the opportunity of going back and examining the experience, digesting it, and reveals those elements lost or overlooked in the fleeting moments of the actual experience, giving insights that would otherwise be unavailable.

In addition, photography is, by its nature, closely linked to the art of the drama, wherein it is possible to illuminate not only a human condition in a single photograph, but a human process in a series of images, as feelings are developed, intensified, expressed, shared and changed.

To develop the material for the book I attended several workshops in Wisconsin and California. There are no posed photographs and I used only existing light. I used no extra lights or flash that might interfere with the experience of the participants. I was in each case accepted as a member of the workshop. Everyone knew I was there and why, and agreed to permit me to take the photographs so that they might share the workshop experience with you.

I want to dedicate my work in this book to the many people who helped bring it to fruition. To Elisabeth Kübler-Ross, whose friendship and generosity in allowing me to share in her work made it possible. To the members of the workshop (with a special thank you to Linda Schuman) for their willingness to share the experience, and to my wife Betty Weir, whose vision, help and understanding are very much a part of this work.

Acknowledgments

Since I am—in this life—learning and teaching forgiveness, I want to use this opportunity to thank J. and M. for three years of appreciated assistance in these workshops.

I also want to thank Mal for his continuous support; Sheila and Tom, without whom I could not have continued so easily, Linda and Lynn for holding the fort during my absences from Shanti Nilaya; the many participants of the workshops who have enriched our lives by their courage and sharing; and last but not least, the Divine Guidance which alone makes this work possible.

ELISABETH K. ROSS

Working It Through

1
David

❧❧

I N   A   S E N S E , this book starts at the end.

It starts with the story of David. It also starts with someone else's writing and someone else's words, rather than mine. When I was first asked to write a book about the hundreds of Life, Death and Transition Workshops I have given all over the world over the past ten years, I thought, "Where can I begin?" Soon the answer came to me. Do not start at the beginning. Start at the end. Do not attempt to explain in the very first chapter how this work began, how these workshops came into being, how they function and operate, etc. Start with the end, with the *results* of these workshops.

And so this book begins by telling you about the end product of our workshops. And by telling you about the end of David's life. Endings, someone once wrote, are just beginnings backwards. That is nowhere more true than it is here.

Following is a letter written to me by David's mother. It will tell you a lot about why this book is called *Working It Through*.

Dear Elisabeth: May 1, 1979

6:00 A.M.—the beginning of a new day. May Basket Day! When I was a little girl, we got up early to pick cowslips and violets for the baskets of popcorn and fudge we placed by our friends' front door. But you have asked me to remember a more recent time—the workshop, and what it meant to me and my family. Oh, Elisabeth, how can I even begin to put that into words? The workshop opened a whole new world for all of us to live in! I want to tell everybody about it. But to do that I will have to think back to those awful days, and it hurts so much to remember. I would rather think about Val's wedding in our garden next month. David and Brad look so tall and handsome in their new suits. Dave is practicing the songs he will sing. There is excitement in our house. New memories to mix with the old. Some of the old memories I don't want to think about, but today I must. I have stolen this whole day from a hectic week to write about the workshop. So I will sit quietly and remember—

"You are ruining your life trying to take care of me, Mom."

"Oh, no, David. Please don't say that. I love you so much." (Oh, Lord, he knows. I have tried to hide my desperation, but David knows. I just can't do it anymore. Why won't you help me? Why won't somebody help me? Please— please—)

That was only the beginning of a conversation between my son and me. The next morning I obtained Dr. Ross's address from our public library. I wrote to her, pouring out my feelings about our eighteen-year-old son, David, who has had surgery twice for brain tumors and was left with facial paralysis, repeated corneal ulcers, impairment of right-hand movement, poor balance and difficulty walking and partial deafness. He has seizures and takes four kinds of medication daily. There is another tumor growing. David has always been a very special human being with so much to give. But most people are afraid because of his handicaps or too busy to really get to know him. So he has no friends and the world is a lonely place. He accepted that, making music and his guitar his friends. His room was his safe, warm place, filled with music, his artwork, laughter and love. Now he felt lonely and unacceptable even here because there was so much tension and weariness in the house. So many tears and not much laughter anymore. Worst of all, the tumor is growing and he knew he would soon be deaf —no more stereo, no more Beatles, no more guitar, no more music. All of his friends would be gone. David has struggled so hard to live with dignity, to learn to respect himself. Now he was telling me he didn't want to go on living anymore.

"David, do you feel that bad? What can I do to help you?"

"There's nothing you can do, Mom. That's just the way it is." And he cried, and he put his arm around me and patted my shoulder. David never cries. "Tears won't do any good, Mom," he always tells me. But he never told me not to cry, so I wept for both of us.

I finished my letter to Elisabeth and asked for help. As I stood in front of the mailbox, I told God that I had done everything I could do and our lives were in His hands. Elisabeth was home one day a week with thousands of letters to answer, but within two weeks I received a letter from her, sending help and hope.

In January 1978 my husband Dave and I attended our first workshop at Shanti Nilaya.* Our daughter had the flu. A blizzard had closed O'Hare Field. But we were meant to be at that workshop and we were. For five days, forty-six people talked and listened to each other. We also laughed, sang and ate together. We shared our fears, guilt and anger. We learned to forgive others and to forgive ourselves. We allowed other human beings to see our tears and pain. We all cared and we showed it.

At this workshop I relived some of the experiences of David's childhood which hurt him so terribly. I shared the guilt I still felt for mistakes made because I was insecure and inexperienced, trusting doctors and so-called experts who were not trustworthy. I shared the heartbreak of hearing David say his life had been worthless, the anguish of watching him try to face living without music, the helplessness of trying to comfort him when there is no hope.

After the privilege of attending two workshops, I wanted David to have that wonderful experience. I knew he had as much to give as he would receive. So I wrote to Elisabeth, but she didn't answer. Then on a Thursday in August, she called, asking if we could bring David to a workshop in California the following Monday. I said yes without even thinking how impossible it would be to make all the arrangements in three days or how I could take him two thousand miles from home by myself, against his doctor's advice. I knew it

---

* This is our center in Escondido, California, about which we will tell more later.

was meant to be, and with the help of a lot of good people, it happened.

When we came out for breakfast the first morning, there was the usual reaction to David. He is impressive! Six feet tall with a red Afro and a red beard. The right side of his face droops because of the paralysis. His right eyelid is sewn shut. He walks with his legs far apart to balance himself. And he is deaf. Some of the people were uncomfortable. Some were afraid. But soon, they began to come closer, to communicate with him. To every person who reached out to him, he gave his unconditional love.

I didn't know how David would react to sitting all day in a room full of people when he couldn't hear what they said. I took a notebook and tried to summarize for him what every person was sharing with the group. From the very beginning he was completely absorbed in the feelings being expressed. He willingly shared his own. "My name is David," he said. "I have come to get help." During the breaks he looked longingly at the swimming pool, remembering how he loved to swim. On Tuesday some of the men took him in the pool, the first time in over two years. He had a ball! When asked if he had come with any special answer to find, his reply was "Yes, myself." In the evening John, the priest, was saying mass out on a huge rock. David looked up and saw the big ankh silhouetted against the sky. I told him it was the symbol of life. I gave him the one I had on a chain. It became very important to him, and he has worn it ever since.

Thursday morning David told me, "Mrs. Ross has a lot of people to do, and I probably won't get done, but I would like to tell the people that I have trouble with praying." He asked if John, the priest, could help him because "he is good at praying."

So David shared: "I have trouble with praying."

John wrote: "Tell me what you want to pray for."

The answer was: "For knowing God."

John wrote: "When we love one another, we feel God. We are now praying to God."

The room was very quiet. Then suddenly everyone surrounded David, hugging him and each other. David knew God! He felt the joy of sharing himself and of feeling the love of the group and the love of God. Through his sharing, many people realized that God is love. David is a precious gift to all of us.

So we came home. In September David's great-aunt was dying of cancer and she was afraid. She wrote to David often. He had a cross and chain which he was saving for me. He wrapped it with a note and sent his dad and me to put it around her neck. His note said, "Love this as I do mine. I think it will open your heart toward your new life." She never took it off. It symbolized all the love that surrounded her. On September 25 she died peacefully and unafraid.

David continues to give unconditional love to all who reach out to him. He takes care of his roommate, who can't walk or talk or read or write. It makes our hearts sing to watch the special kind of communication they share.

In March I was asked to speak to five classes of high school seniors—sharing with them what it is like for a family to face death; our feelings, how we cope and how the workshops have helped us. A year ago I would have been too scared to consider such a request and my husband would have had to drive me if I went. Yet there I was, alone on the expressway during the rush hour in a snowstorm! I didn't think of backing out and I wasn't afraid because living without fear and sharing is what the workshops are all about. I hoped to show these students that even in the face of death, it is possible to enjoy life. I talked about the things we do together. I read them some of David's poems and answered their questions. We shared our feelings. It was a special time for me.

We see David every Wednesday, Friday and Saturday. He is home for birthdays, holidays and all special days. When he is able, he attends a special school for the physically handicapped and a sheltered workshop. He is deaf now, blind in one eye. He doesn't want any more surgery, and we agree with his decision. He is not afraid. Communication is very slow, mostly in writing with some sign language. Hugging is the best way and we do a lot of that. Sometimes our grief overwhelms us and we have to cry, but we also laugh and love and enjoy each day. Love will be with us forever!

We are a family. Today there are five of us. We don't know about tomorrow.

Both Dave (my husband) and I learned from the sisters and brothers of other terminally ill patients who attended your workshop. We listened to their feelings of rejection and anger toward their parents, the guilt and pain they suffered. We realized that we are only human parents and can't do it all. Understanding this, we considered our own needs and those of our other two children. Our tremendous burden of guilt lifted, making it possible for us to live in peace with the heartbreaking decision of nursing-home care for David.

This workshop was one of the most joyful experiences Dave and I have ever shared in our thirty-two years of marriage.

In February Elisabeth made a house call to meet David and talk with him. His own words say it all: "Mrs. Ross lifted my heart. She gave me peace."

David's mother attended another workshop, her last, alone a year ago. Here is what she had to say about it:

6:00 A.M. May 9th. My mom's birthday. She died of cancer in 1974, three weeks before David had his first brain surgery. The grief I had to postpone then was one of the reasons I needed another workshop. In the spring of 1978 my physical health deteriorated under the weight of additional responsibilities. There were just too many problems in my life that I could do nothing about. The world was going blithely by my door while I struggled along. Nobody really cared—not even God. My exhaustion turned to anger, and I was like a block of ice, trying not to feel anything. I asked Elisabeth to let me come to the June workshop in Wisconsin but it was already full. I was scared to go alone, but I needed help fast and I knew I would get it at the workshop. So I bugged Elisabeth until she said yes.

In Wisconsin the volcano erupted and I let out my anger toward a lot of things and a lot of people. Most of all toward myself for not being the person I really wanted to be all my life because I was afraid. I told God what a big bully he was and what I thought of him for not helping his children—all of this in front of more than seventy people, ten of whom were clergy. After surviving that, I convinced myself that I wasn't afraid of anything anymore. What a relief!

In December 1980 David had pneumonia with complications and was near death, but our family still needed him to help us so he stayed with us for a little while longer. He died suddenly on March 7, 1981. We were with him and we are thankful that we had been able to work through our guilt and fear so when the time came, we could let him go in peace.

When David was a little boy, he would jump on our bed at 6:00 A.M. and say, "I want to tell you a secret, Mom. I love you with all my heart." From the day he was born, he was always full of love, and he gave it freely to everyone. We were privileged to be his parents. We loved him deeply and it hurt so much to give him back to God. His beautiful spirit will always be with us whenever we feel love.

I now want to add a little postscript of my own to the story of David as told by his mother. I will start by saying that David's physician had strongly discouraged the parents' request for permission to take David to our Life, Death and Transition Workshop. It was regarded as an imposition and as a totally impossible task. Both parents listened to their own intuition and, over the objections of the medical team, his mom brought him anyway. As it turned out, it was the first time in David's life that he had had five days with his mom all alone without having to share her with his siblings. It was the first time he began to understand her pain, her grief and her problems in an open and honest way.

It is important to add that the mother, due to much of

her guilt and unresolved shame over her inability and un-readiness to listen to David, tried to protect him. She had a tendency to sit next to him and to hover over him. David emerged out of this workshop as a rather independent spirit, separating himself on his own initiative from the clinging mother, who finally was able to let go of him.

We all watched him with a sense of pride as he requested a swim in the pool, something he had not done for years and had enjoyed in his healthier days. With the help of other strong workshop participants he was carried into the pool and enjoyed an hour of fun and joy in the element of his choice. It seems that under what we would call "normal" circumstances, the last thing in the world one would do with a terminal patient is to take him for a dip in the pool, yet within the framework of the workshop it was the in-telligent, warm, marvelous thing to do, which was beneficial to everybody concerned.

My last good-bye with David was a big, strong hug and a thank-you beyond words—a thank-you not just from David to me, but from me to David for having the courage to attend an exhausting and physically draining five days and nights. It was a thank-you for his willingness to share his experiences with a group of people who also learned one of the hardest lessons—to listen to someone who can barely speak, who is barely audible and who makes it at times very difficult not just to switch off when it becomes too cum-bersome and painful. It was the reaction of the workshop participants to David, and especially his profound question about God at the end of the workshop, and the beautiful and loving response of the priest that makes these encounters so unforgettable.

It is not enough to say that David stayed in touch with many of the workshop participants and that he very occa-sionally even sent me a love letter. This in itself was an incredible gift, considering how long it took him to write a single word on a piece of paper. But at the moment of his death he knew with pride and joy that he had touched many lives.

This, in the end, is what our Life, Death and Transition Workshops are all about. Touching lives.

2
The First Workshops

AFTER I LEFT THE UNIVERSITY of Chicago, where I had started the first interdisciplinary seminar on the care of dying patients, I was invited to many talk shows, television appearances and especially lectures. At first the lectures were to nursing schools, nursing homes, medical schools, seminaries and funeral director organizations, but later to a great number of other interested organizations, with an increasing demand from the general public.

It became clear that even while traveling a quarter of a million miles a year for ten years and reaching approximately fifteen thousand people a week, we only scratched the surface. We were able to share verbally with a great number of people the process of dying; the difficulties the patient faces; the anxieties, fears and inhibitions of family members, and also of staff whose own fears and anxieties interfered with the most effective work. But this one-way sharing did not seem enough. It did not touch the problem, it only described it.

It was in 1970 that the thought occurred to me that I was ready to choose a relatively small group of people to work with in more depth. I would spend a whole week with them in a live-in retreat and experiment with the desire to share with them more than just verbal communications. I wanted o have more time with them and allow them to experience what it is like when our own negativity, our own fears and unfinished business, interferes with our effectiveness.

INDIANA WORKSHOP

Sixty people were picked at random from a large number who expressed an interest. We rented a lovely retreat place out in the country in Indiana where we met from Monday until Friday and shared whatever we were willing and able to share of our own experiences with living and dying. The group consisted of a number of nurses, clergy from different denominations, two funeral directors, one other physician, several terminally ill patients and a cross section of professionals indirectly responsible for patient care, as well as a number of bereaved people.

We had no program, no schedule. We simply met early in the morning right after breakfast, started singing to the accompaniment of a guitar, shared a few moments of silence to recollect our thoughts. Then I proceeded to share some of the difficulties patients face when, suspicious of a potential terminal illness, they submit to a medical checkup and receive, or do not receive, the information they sometimes desperately seek, sometimes hope to avoid.

One patient present instantly started to share her experience at this phase of her illness, how she was not dealt with openly and frankly. Other patients shared how they were faced with too much frankness when they were not ready to hear "the truth." And so within a very short period of time on the first day, we became involved in very meaningful and emotional dialogue and sharing about the very beginning of the experience of "becoming a patient with a potentially terminal illness."

Without any real planning, the week proceeded in a

natural evolution of a process very similar to the one experienced by terminally ill patients as they move from the awareness of their diagnosis to their final acceptance or resignation just prior to death. The first day dealt mainly with the issues of denial, with playing games, questions of honesty and sharing, with all the aspects that prevent people from open communication—their own fears, anxieties, shame, guilt, negative memories and conditioning. It involved staff, family members and patients, all of whom were present in a natural random selection of our first one-week workshop.

The second day much anger surfaced, often directed at the physician, who triggered a lot of negative feelings that the participants harbored within themselves. Through the course of the day they became aware of their own projections, their own displacements and ultimately their own unfairness in putting every professional into the mold of their own negative experiences.

By Wednesday much grief, many tears, were shed, and much anger was displayed. But the evening sessions, which always started with singing and music, brought the group together as a whole.

The most moving aspect of this first group experience was the willingness of young and old to share their most intimate pain, fears and anxieties without worrying what the other person might think of them. Each time one of them shared their pain, it triggered off tears, guilt, shame or anger in the other participants, who slowly and gradually became aware of their own unfinished business, which they were later able to share with the group.

BARBARA

My own daughter, at that time eight years old, participated in the workshop as the youngest member. This was also unplanned. Because of the snowfall of the preceding winter the school vacation was advanced one week and I gave both of my children the option to either join my first Life, Death and Transition Workshop or to spend the week at home in the absence of their mother, something I had never done before for such a length of time, My eleven-year-old son chose to stay home with his friends while Barbara joined me in my first adventure with a group. She stayed close to two of the people she already knew—Sheryl, a music therapist for terminally ill children, and Vicki, a beautiful nurse from Indiana. Sheryl and Vicki were both comfortable with the topic of death and dying and with children.

It was a great delight to see how a child was able to be included in such an emotional, intense one-week workshop without the need to escape even though the long sessions often lasted till way after midnight. On a few occasions Barbara took a walk during the breaks and shared some of her personal feelings, mainly with Sheryl; most of the time she felt quite comfortable sharing with the whole group, and exhibited a wisdom that sometimes made me think of a wise old lady in the body of a young child.

I think this was my first awareness that even my own children, though we never discussed much of my work at home, were quite familiar with my basic philosophy. It naturally gave me a feeling of contentment and satisfaction to know that I was not only going out to "preach to the world," but that some of it was rubbing off in my household without my explicitly talking about it or making it a point to try to "teach" my ideas.

ANGRY YOUNG MINISTER

One of the most moving memories of my first workshop, and in some ways perhaps the most significant event of that week, was the sharing of a young, angry minister from

Indiana. He was most beloved by the group but was unable to verbalize much of his pain although it was written all over his face and his body. On Wednesday evening I challenged him to "spit out" some of his repressed rage and anger, which was poorly disguised. He finally blurted out with a tremendous amount of emotion that he was sick and tired of all the talk of the dying patients and their family members and the people who had lost a child, that they were lucky that they were dead, that this was a very small issue. The real issue, he said, was something that we never discussed in this workshop and was a thousand times worse than anything we ever brought up.

He then shared the fact that his young wife had left him, had taken his two young children. Their marriage had fallen apart, and from a very proud young father and husband, and very much appreciated minister in the community, he suddenly felt like an outcast, a black sheep, a bachelor—but not by choice! The pain, agony and grief of losing these children without the possibility of having said good-bye to them was far worse than the death experience. It also challenged his "public image" as a minister, an example to the parish—but this became a secondary issue at this point.

I had no problem empathizing with him, but wondered if this split happened so suddenly that he had never had a chance to talk with his children. When I asked why he had never done that prior to the physical separation, it was obvious that he had no words, no real understanding of the comprehension of preschool children in a separation of this kind. His main grief, coupled with his grief over his inability to reconcile with his wife, was that his parish and his ministerial work had taken so much time out of his life that he never took time out to share some of this pain and sense of loss with his two preschool children.

Since the youngsters lived within driving distance from our retreat place, I challenged him to drive home the same night and show up the next morning with the two children. I was willing to include the five- and seven-year-olds in our workshop, assisted mainly by my eight-year-old daughter. This would give him the opportunity to share with his children his care, love, grief and pain. Then if the court eventually decided that they had to go with their mother, at least the children would have the memory of those two days and would always know the depth of his love and care.

I then separated from him briefly to talk with another patient, and when I returned to the dining room he was gone. I did not pay much attention to this until I noticed that he was not present for the evening session. Lo and behold, he was there at breakfast with two children on his lap, happily eating, giggling and laughing, hugging and communicating with them as he had never done before.

The children sat through the Thursday and Friday sessions and listened very attentively to all the sharing of the grown-ups. When the minister left on Friday with his two children, he was beaming all over and had a great sense of confidence that no matter what happened, his children would have a very, very special memory.

A few months later I received a phone call from him with the incredible news that the judge had seen his two children in chambers and had decided that the children would be assigned to him since it was the children's choice! The love and the care that the three of them had for each other became so obvious that the judge felt he had no choice but to give custody of the children to the father. All this occurred in 1970, when such a decision was still very rare.

This was perhaps a small matter, considering the very deep emotional traumas and experiences—particularly those involving loss through the death of a loved one—with which we deal in these workshops, but it opened up a whole new avenue. We became aware that these workshops are relevant to the huge number of people who go through a great variety of griefs, pains and losses. It probably made the whole group aware that it is not death that is the ultimate loss, but the separation from loved ones. Knowing about their continued existence but unable to share it with them may cause far more pain and make a resolution far more difficult than a permanent physical separation through death.

Another beautiful event of that first workshop was again with my own daughter, Barbara. On the last day when it was time to leave and everybody wanted a hug and a little extra private time, my daughter came up to me very resolutely and said, "I need fifteen minutes with you alone." I told her that we were going to have a three-hour drive back to Flossmoor together, but she was not satisfied with that and again said she needed to see me alone right now, with the emphasis on "right now." Needless to say, I couldn't help but remember my own teachings of a few days earlier when I shared with the group that when a patient says they need to see you *right now,* they mean right now and not tomorrow. I had to smile to myself, knowing or becoming aware, of how difficult it is to practice what we preach to others. Before I could answer her, she added another condition to our private time. She said, "I want you to sneak out through the back door so nobody grabs you again."

And so very obediently and curiously, I sneaked out through the back door of the retreat place and followed as she ran up the hill through some underbrush in the forest. To my great surprise we ended up in an incredibly beautiful old cemetery. It was so totally covered by greenery that I had not been aware of its presence during the whole week. She went straight to a specific gravestone and with her wise old woman manner said, "All I need to know from you is what you think about that"—pointing to the writing on the gravestone. On the gravestone were four names—a mother, a father and two children. Two of them had obviously died, as the years of their births and deaths were engraved in the stone. One of the parents and a child were apparently still alive as there were only their names and birth years, and the other space was left open.

I looked at it briefly, and being tired of talking for a whole week about death and dying, ready to switch gears and go home, I said to her very spontaneously, "I think this is going a bit too far. I think they could easily wait to put their names on the gravestone until they are dead. Enough is enough." Before I could add any more she gave a big sigh of relief, hugged me, laughed and said, "Thank you. That's all I wanted to know," and ran down the hill to the car, ready to go home.

On the drive home I realized again the beauty of the symbolic language of children. Here was an eight-year-old girl who, unplanned and really quite unprepared, joined us at the last minute in an adult, intense and highly emotional five days and nights of talking about death and dying. The question obviously occurred to her whether Mom would know where to stop, or would she go home now and order some gravestones with the names of the four family members and wait until one of us would die so we could finish the carvings. It was a very simple and beautiful nonverbal communication asking whether there was an end to the preparation for death, whether we were able to switch gears now and go back home to the living. My answer obviously satisfied her and the issue was closed, as it is so quickly for children, who do not carry such ruminations along with them as grown-ups do.

Out of this week in Richmond, Indiana, came many deep and lasting friendships for myself and for the other participants—and especially for the terminally ill patients who suddenly sensed that they had a support system where they had none before. Workshop participants continued to call on them, to write to them, to keep in touch with them and remember anniversaries or special dates. Many also were willing to share the final days or hours with them if they should need additional nursing care or simply moral support. Many of these patients shared with me the great sense of security in knowing that after leaving the workshop they have support even if their family should desert them or become apprehensive or frantic. They appreciated having a support system that they could call upon day and night.

My own daughter deepened her friendship with Sheryl, who became like an older sister to her, a friendship that has continued to grow. Now that my daughter is a teenager they still relate to each other as two sisters, an important thing for a girl who had always wanted a sister.

What this workshop taught me is that five-day live-in retreats are not only possible but mandatory. They are a natural evolution, not only in learning more about the care of dying patients, but also in our own emotional growth work which is necessary in order for us to be able to work with critically ill patients or people in any kind of crisis.

OHIO WORKSHOP

I remember vividly also an early workshop in Ohio where a nun asked if I would honor their convent by having my retreat under their roof. They had decided that their many beautiful convent acres were not being used and that they were willing to open their gates, homes, grounds and chapel to workshop participants to deal with an issue congruent to their philosophy and teachings. This St. Francis retreat was on an enormously large and beautiful property, although the main house looked cold and sterile, and was inhabited mainly by elderly sisters who still wore their habits. They were used to serenity, peace and quiet, and not to a group of laughing, singing, giggling, crying and angry people who needed a place where they could externalize and share a lot of pain.

Our first encounter at this convent was rather dramatic. I myself drove to Ohio, something I had never done before, with two nuns in the backseat of my car. We sang all the way from Chicago to Ohio, to stay awake, and arrived, unfortunately at 1:00 A.M. We knocked at many doors at the convent, including the door of the priest who still had his light on. He simply looked through the curtain and refused to let us in. We made a remarkable amount of noise and disturbance before one of the older sisters finally came out, half-sleepy and rather reluctant, obviously not happy with the late arrival, and showed us to some rooms.

The next morning when we came to breakfast, I automatically lit a cigarette and a dozen sisters, average age about seventy-five, jumped up very annoyed and made it very clear that smoking was not permissible on these premises!

After breakfast they showed us the conference room, which was a very cold rectangular lecture hall with stiff metal folding chairs, a blackboard and a speaker's desk in the front. This was an acceptable place for a lecture, but certainly not feasible for intimate and very emotional sharing—especially with the nuns' bedrooms right above it!

I had a discussion with the mother superior to explain that this room was unacceptable, and asked for alternatives. The grounds were enormous and there were many buildings that were much more warm and cozy which would encourage true sharing, away from the house of the sisters, where we would obviously interfere with their usual quiet life-style.

Some very young novices came enthusiastically and asked if we would do them a great favor. It was their big dream that they would once be allowed to spend a few days in the main house with "the real sisters" and they would be more than thrilled to lend us the house of the novices if we wouldn't mind the rather closed-in quarters, the small living room and the cluttered space. We went to investigate their home and found it filled with pictures, love, flowers, pillows and couches. Although crowded it looked like a warm, cozy, beautiful home and just the right kind of living room atmosphere that we needed to sit together in a circle and share our joys and our pain.

To my great surprise the mother superior was not only willing to make this swap but appeared personally with fifty ashtrays in her arms to make sure we were comfortable. She assured us they would be willing to do anything in their power to make this workshop a success not only for us but for them, since it was the first time they had opened their house to outsiders. Our difficult beginning became a successful mutual experience through our open communicating, through our sharing our needs and requests with them and their willingness to be flexible and allow things that were not previously permissible on their premises.

One of our next problems was the presence of two rabbis who ate only kosher meals, We didn't quite know how to tell the mother superior that we needed kosher food brought into this Catholic convent. But again, as with the issue of the smoking and the ashtrays, there was no objection and they were willing to bend backwards to accommodate all our needs. This was not easy in a small community in Ohio where they did not even have a delicatessen in town.

On Thursday evening, our last evening at this Catholic retreat place, we were so in love with the sisters that we invited all of them, including the novices who gave us their own private home for the week, to come and join us in a sing-along around our campfire outside. Many of the sisters stood next to the fire and sang solos for us; several composed songs for us, and we in turn composed a song for them. We sang our appreciation for the nuns of this convent, who made us feel at home and shared with unconditional love, who helped us all to learn what it could be if we would live as brothers and sisters together without discriminating and putting people into molds.

Since we had decided to have our own bread and wine for that Thursday-night ritual, we also ran into a problem which none other than the mother superior became aware of. Just as we lit the fire, she came running to me and said with a gasp of despair, "My dear, we forgot to buy some kosher wine!" Before I could think where in the world we would get kosher wine in this tiny community in Ohio, she and another sister dashed off and soon returned triumphantly bearing two bottles of kosher wine just in time for the ritual. We laughed about this and wondered what their priest would say if he was aware of it, he who had been so upset about our late arrival.

There were many beautiful memories from this workshop. But I think the highlight was that a group of nuns who had lived a rather restricted life very much apart from the outside world, were open, caring and loving enough to make it possible for a rabbi to fall in love with a nun. Everyone shared not only the pains and the joys of this workshop, but again many friendships were started which have lasted until the present time. The rabbi and the nun still write to each other. We still hear from the nuns at Easter and Christmas, and naturally on St. Francis day, and their open invitation to any of the workshop participants has been upheld during the many years that we have not seen each other.

An incredible, very sad footnote to this workship was the fact that we were informed only on the very last day that the top floor of this convent was filled with old, retired, crippled, handicapped, incapacitated and dying nuns. When we learned this, we naturally immediately went to visit them, and many a tear was shed by these nuns when they heard what we had been doing there all week. Had we known earlier, we would have brought them down to participate in our workshop even if we had to bring them on stretchers or in wheelchairs. It was an important lesson for everyone there to know that even in a place of love like this, there is a tendency to hide those people, to keep them away, out of fear that they may upset us or we may upset them.

These retreats in Indiana and Ohio were two of our *earliest workshops*. Because of their success, we began planning more workshops. Needless to say, both the number and the size of these workshops has increased ever since. Having held workshops all over the world now, we have discovered that they are beneficial for people of all different ages, cultures, religions and professional backgrounds. Hundreds of lay people who have attended these retreats simply for their own growth and for feeling more comfortable dealing with natural life crises in their own family have been joined by twice as many professionals, clergy, nurses, physicians, therapists and lawyers.

Each workshop that we scheduled from the early days took place in a different state, in a different retreat center. I commuted from state to state simply to make them available to as many people as possible. I wanted to include indigent people, and especially cancer patients, who had already depleted all their financial resources for doctor and hospital bills and who were not financially able to fly across the country to attend. It became a simple matter of finding the right kind of retreat place.

We needed a place out in the country, housing where we would be left alone, where no other groups were also meeting, with simple but adequate accommodations and acceptable food. We needed a spot where we could share the meals together and where nobody would be disturbed when our session lasted until 1, 2, or 3 in the morning, and with a coffeepot and a teapot available day and night. We needed room for people to wander off and roam around the premises when they needed a certain distance from material too emotional for them to deal with at the immediate time. We wanted a place far enough from a town that people were not tempted to "go to the bar at night," or to go shopping or attend to other distractions that would dilute the experience and "make it easier on them."

The centers were as different as the people who ran them. Some of them were stiff and uptight, inflexible, and we vowed never to go back to those places. Others were full of warmth, love and care. In each one we invited one of the staff people to participate in the workshop as a guest, in order to leave a gift behind us.

Our choice retreats were usually religious retreats simply because they more often met these criteria. These retreats are usually built on large acreage, which gave us the freedom to have some sessions outdoors, or to form small groups during our very limited free time, to share privately in personal encounters or sometimes to have small discussion groups about special issues such as euthanasia, the hospice movement, suicide or other relevant subtopics. Many of these convents had a special kind of security and spirituality that enhanced our sharing manyfold.

WORKSHOPS INCREASE WITH NEED AND DEMAND

The number of participants increased as the range in ages increased, until we had workshops where the youngest was eleven years old and the oldest was ninety-two. What happened frequently is that middle-aged working people would attend a workshop, and then give an invitation to one or both of their parents as a Christmas gift. The parents would then offer it as a Christmas gift to their grandchildren, thus making it possible for us to get to know three or four generations of a family over the period of two or three years. Once a wife attended a workshop, she invariably would try to convince her husband to come the following year. Once both mates had attended the workshop, they would send on relatives whom they felt had the need to work on unfinished business. We have never advertised any of these workshops, but for each participant we had we received between three and five new registrations.

At one time we had fifteen hundred people on the waiting list for the following year, until we increased the workshops and literally spread them all over the world.

3

Shanti Nilaya—"Home of Peace"

❧❧

IT BECAME OBVIOUS very soon that I could no longer handle alone the task that I had taken on, Not only had the number of workshop participants increased, with the waiting lists growing longer and longer; now people started to send hospital staff members from as far away as Australia. Many, especially those who traveled thousands of miles, expressed an urgent need to have further training beyond the five-day intensive workshops.

For myself, I could not even think about offering such training at this point in time. It was enough for me simply to handle seventy to eighty people at a workshop twice a month. I was growing very tired; becoming very depleted of energy.

I remember vividly a workshop in Santa Barbara where I was exhausted on the last evening when everybody decided to have a party in one of the dormitories. I watched enviously as they all went to the music hall for singing, sharing, dancing and backrubs, and I was preoccupied with a number of people who were critically ill. Neither they nor I could participate in many of these fun activities of our last evening together.

It was five o'clock in the morning when I finally returned to my own room, determined to sleep for two hours before the breakfast bell rang for our last Friday morning get-together. On the last morning we usually deal with the issues of letting go and saying good-bye. Before I had fallen asleep, one of the nurses dashed into my room, all excited, and begged me to share her birthday with her by watching the sunrise out my window. I told her that I wasn't aware that it was her birthday, and she quickly said that it was not her actual birthday, but that it was like a rebirth experience to be free of guilt and fear and that she regarded this very day as the beginning of a totally new life.

The last thing I remember telling her is that she was invited to watch the sunrise out of my bedroom window but that I was too exhausted to participate physically. I told her I would be with her "in spirit" if she would allow me the peace of sleeping for two hours and be willing to wake me up at seven o'clock in the morning to join the rest of the group for our last breakfast.

I then drifted off into a deep, trancelike sleep during which time I had my first out-of-body experience, a phenomenon I was totally and completely unfamiliar with—I did not even know the term *out-of-body* at that time. I saw myself lifted out of my physical body. As I described it later, it was as if a whole lot of loving beings were taking all the tired parts out of me, similar to car mechanics in a car repair shop. It was as if they were replacing every tired and worn-out part of my physical body with a new, fresh, energized part. I experienced a great sense of peace and serenity, a feeling of literally being taken care of, of having no worry in the world. I had also an incredible sense that once all the parts were replaced, I would be as young and fresh and energetic as I had been prior to this rather exhausting, draining workshop.

When I woke up two hours later, prior to the ringing of the bell, I felt incredibly energized. I jumped off my bed as if I had had nine hours of sleep, and looked with great amazement at the nurse who stood there with a knowing smile and very matter-of-factly informed me that I must have had a real out-of-body experience. I told her that I did not know what she was talking about, but shared my experience with her. She referred me to the library, where I could read up on this interesting phenomenon. Naturally I associated this immediately with the stories of dying patients who shared with me their near-death experiences. They had described how they were lifted or floated out of their physical body into a timeless and spaceless existence where they were often prepared for their transition, where they were surrounded with loving care, and where they had no fears or anxieties.

I was most excited about this personal experience and could barely wait until the workshop was over so I could go to the Santa Barbara library (and soon after to the library in San Francisco) to search for literature on out-of-body experiences. It was there that I found Robert Monroe's book, *Journeys out of the Body.* It is a rather boring and dull text. Nevertheless, it is probably the best book written on the phenomenon of the out-of-body experience for a layman like me. I did not know what this experience was and desperately searched for explanations and descriptions of this strange occurrence that most people would not associate with reality in those days.

Little did we know then that that was the beginning of an enormous amount of new research, which ultimately led to the understanding of death and life after death.

By the fall of 1976 I had reached the point where I began to realize that I could not continue this work alone any longer. I had for the past decade lectured and traveled, held workshops across the United States, Europe, Canada, South America and Japan and had seen innumerable patients in between. My correspondence started to pile up and I was forever thousands of letters behind. Although I hired two secretarial assistants, it was never possible to catch up with the backlog of correspondence. What became even more evident was the increased need for these intense, live-in workshops. My reserve energy decreased.

The workshop previous to the one in Santa Barbara had been held in Canada, with seventy participants, including a quadriplegic, several cancer patients and some rather disturbed, borderline psychotic patients. We worked until midnight the first night, two o'clock the second night, three o'clock the third night and until 5:00 A.M. the last night of the workshop, always beginning the work at 9:00 A.M. When I completed the five-day, live-in retreat, I was depleted and exhausted physically from lack of sleep. And although I enjoyed the tremendous sharing and caring especially of this given group, I felt that I needed a week to recuperate before I was able to go "on the road again."

It was after this workshop that I admitted my need for help and henceforth always brought one or two assistants with me. Requests started to come in from different members of the helping professions for more individual and longer-term training. This seemed an impossible task, as I had a hectic travel schedule, which never allowed me more than a day or two in one given place. I also see patients all over the world. I was spending much time in consultations, interpretations of drawings of dying children and giving general guidelines for parents, schoolteachers, clergy and counselors. It was impossible for me to take on trainees, or for that matter medical students, for a few months of externships to train them in this very special and newly evolving field of medicine.

The big dream naturally became more and more crystallized in my mind: to have a place of our own, somewhere in the mountains, I hoped, which remind me of my childhood. We wanted a place with the peace and serenity of a mountain area, yet accessible to all those who were seeking help. We needed adequate access by road and an airport not too terribly far away for those who were terminally ill or handicapped and unable to take long-distance car trips.

We spent time making searches in the mountains of Escondido, fantasizing what it would be like if we could actually find a large piece of land. We could open up a retreat center where we could train staff in this kind of work, a place where people, especially those who came from far away, could stay and live while attending our Life, Death and Transition Workshops. A place where people would come simply to get in touch with their own negativity and relieve their pain, their anguish, their agony and their anger, to emerge free and purified and able to live life more positively and more fully.

It was on one of these walks that we came to a piece of land that was not for sale, but that not only looked attractive but filled one with an incredible peace and serenity. It was a plateau of forty-two acres on top of a mountain, surrounded by a circle of boulder-covered mountains. We saw a beautiful blue sky above, orange trees, an occasional avocado tree, wild lilac bushes and the typical vegetation of southern California. There had been years of drought, and much of it was yellow and dry; but there was a very special serenity in this place, which we had not seen in any of the places that had a "for sale" sign.

What could we lose by asking the owner if he had any intention of selling? Since we didn't have any money, it was more a pursuit of a dream than anything else. We were met by an extremely lovely and hospitable British lady and her very gallant and lovable husband, who introduced us to some of their pretty, grown-up daughters. We simply shared our dream with him. He made it clear very quickly that he had anticipated selling his piece of land since all his children were grown, and he and his wife did not need forty-two acres, which required more work than he was able to put into it. Since he lived and worked and earned his living at home, it was simple for him to find another place nearby or near some of his married children, and he was seriously considering selling the property if he found the right buyer.

We were very honest and very open with him. We told him we had no idea where the money would come from, but that we also knew that this was the right kind of land and somehow the money would be provided. I have no idea what he thought of us. He probably regarded us as a bunch of fantasizing idealists (which in a sense we are), but he was always cordial and kind to us.

Two weeks later, when we returned, a car was there with prospective buyers who had money in cash available to pay for the property immediately. We again asked the owner to save this land for us, since it simply felt right and on some level of awareness we knew that this would be the right property.

Our biggest problem was to find enough money to make a down payment. The only way I knew of to do that was to go to a bank where I had a good credit rating and ask them for a bank loan to buy a piece of property. I was promptly turned down, since there is apparently a bank law that they cannot lend money on out-of-state property.

Very difficult months followed, and my only solution was to appeal to those I had helped in the past. I wrote a letter to all the people who had ever participated in one of my one-week workshops, addressed and stamped a thousand envelopes, and took them all to the Flossmoor post office. I hoped that somewhere, somehow, somebody would give us enough money to make a down payment on Shanti Nilaya.

The letters started coming in, full of love, full of support and encouragement, a lot of lovely thoughts and ideas, but very little cash. Every dollar bill that came was neatly stacked away and put in a special metal box marked "Shanti Nilaya." Every time I flew to California, we made our rounds to the local banks to see if we would be able to get some money from them. The treatment we received was incredibly rude. I am not sure whether it was my own naive approach, whether it was the fact that I was an unknown, strange woman who asked for a large amount of money or whether it was a general philosophy of not lending money to people from out of state, but there was little hope at the end of my search that we would ever obtain enough of a loan to buy the property.

It was on the last day before closing escrow that a letter came in the mail from a group of dying children from Rhode Island. They wrote that they were happy to contribute to Shanti Nilaya, knowing full well that they would never live long enough to profit from it. They had decided to empty their piggy banks of their nickels and dimes and asked their priest to count the money and make a check available to us in the amount of $3.96. When I showed the letter and the check to the owner of the property, whose daughter-in-law was familiar with my work, we were assured that they would keep the property until the money was available. They would save this very special piece of land for us, and they kept their word. They not only kept their word, but they left many valuable items for our use, including some beds, bedsheets, and household articles, which were of a great help to us "beginners."

The dedication of Shanti Nilaya took place on Thanksgiving Sunday morning, November 27, 1977, at sunrise. To our great amazement over a thousand people came from all across the country. Some came in wheelchairs, some in cars and motorcycles, many came in chartered buses, to celebrate the opening of our first, but not last, Shanti Nilaya.

From the top of the rock I gave a welcoming speech at the moment the sun broke out from behind the biggest rocks. Two former workshop participants played on the trumpet "The Impossible Dream," which echoed across the valley and over the mountains, over the crowd of people who were moved and awed by this gift of love of these two people who had never performed in public before. Some well-known singers and musicians played their own creations, and one of our friends sang something from *The Magic Flute*. We had an auction of handmade things that we created during the preceding months to pay for the bills. I had spent the previous six months knitting and crocheting, making pillows, candles and other arts and crafts projects for the opening day. We made exactly enough money to pay for the renting of the school buses, the upkeep of the place, the coffee we served and tents we rented as a portable gift shop. These wonderful people who attended did not hesitate to get up in the wee morning hours to be on top of the mountain at the moment the sun rose and its rays broke through the trees onto the rocks of Shanti Nilaya.

We have since gone through a tremendous amount of turmoil and struggle. After much improvement of the property and upkeep of the road to the top of the mountain, we were refused a special-use permit to build additional facilities that would have allowed us to continue holding our workshops there. This was because the place has no second access road and is regarded as too much of a fire hazard during times of drought. We, naturally, have to accept this decision of the community.

We use this place now as our administrative center and to train the staff for future Shanti Nilayas across the country and abroad; and we still have to rent other retreat places in order to hold our workshops. It is all part of the testing—the tumbler all of us have to go through in life to separate the wheat from the chaff.

There have been many people who wanted to move to California who regarded Shanti Nilaya as a haven or as a future possible commune where they could live. Many of them hoped not to have to work hard to profit from the many teachings that we had anticipated sharing with all those who search. Many left disenchanted because one of the prerequisites for working at Shanti Nilaya is that every single member of my staff, whether he's the gardener or the maintenance man, the medical director or the meditation teacher, has to do his or her own growth work. They have to pass all the tests and the tumbler experiences that all our workshop participants have to go through before they are even considered suitable to staff at a Shanti Nilaya, here or abroad.

Many people who have been counselors for many years think that their academic training is good enough. And when they go through the Life, Death and Transition Workshop, they are awed and stunned by the amount of negativity that emerges. Many are not willing to pay this price of their own growth work for a poorly paid staff position at Shanti Nilaya.

The result of this was naturally a tremendous fall-off of former fans, of people who came with fantasies and dreams of living in a heavenly place on top of a mountain without sharing and giving of themselves.

The separation of the wheat and the chaff is a recurring event. We are now left with a wonderful and dedicated group of people who have been willing to stick it out, to do their own growth work, and who have emerged out of the tumbler as jewels rather than being crushed by it.

We still do not have a place of our own; we are renting the present facilities until we have enough funds to purchase land and build our dream center. We are trying to be patient and to make time our friend!

Meanwhile, people from all over the country and the world often ask at lectures, in telephone calls and letters, "What *is* Shanti Nilaya?" In a column in our newsletter, which goes to more than twenty-five thousand people who have asked to receive it and who want to stay "connected"

with us in other ways, we answered this question. In the
column we said:

The words "Shanti Nilaya" are Sanskrit for
Home of Peace. But that special "home" is not a
particular place. It is not a business, not a corporation, not a group of buildings on a plot of
ground.

Shanti Nilaya is concept, not concrete. That
concept is held in the heart of all who know and
truly understand the meaning of unconditional
love, and who practice it. The concept behind
Shanti Nilaya is that there is a Home of Peace
within each of us. When we go there we are safe,
and unjudged, accepted and loved without condition. When we go there we find enough room
to bring as many into our space of love as there
are people around us. There is always enough
room, and never a scarcity or a lacking.

"Shanti Nilaya" is not a particular place in Escondido, California, or in São Paulo, Brazil, or
in Australia or Holland or on the East Coast. It
is not a multi-national corporation with branch
offices scattered across the map. "Shanti Nilaya"
is beauty, not buildings; grace, not ground; courage, not corporations; compassion, not companies;
love, not legalities; dedication, not doctoral degrees.

It is people loving people. People caring for
others. People growing to know and understand
themselves, and their unique place in the universe.

It is true that much of our work has to do with
the terminally ill, with dying children, with bereaved parents, with others who have suffered
losses in their lives and are dealing with the pain
and the anger and the anxiety of that. Yet it is

larger than that. It has been inspired by an ever enlarging vision and supported by the love of all of you.

We receive many letters from persons asking us how they can become involved in our work in their community. Many of these letter writers tell us they are counselors or hospice organizers, social workers or hospital volunteers, lay ministers and care-givers. And they want to know how they can become "connected" with the mission of Shanti Nilaya.

Of course, we tell them with happiness and joy that they are already doing the work of Shanti Nilaya, and to keep doing it!

And if you are a secretary or an office worker, a policeman or a radio announcer, you, too, are doing the work of Shanti Nilaya if you do what you do out of love, for yourself and others.

The striking fact about Shanti Nilaya is that its largest message can be embraced by people of all religions, backgrounds and experiences, and of all walks of life. You do not have to adopt specific theological doctrines to hear this larger message. You do not even have to be a friend of Shanti Nilaya, because the message is not "ours." It is Universal. And it is beautiful in its simplicity.

There is within each of us a potential for goodness beyond our imagining; for giving which seeks no reward; for listening without judgment; for loving unconditionally.

It is our goal to reach that potential. We can approach it, in ways large and small, every minute of every day, if we try.

When we have found that path, we have built our own "home of peace" inside of ourselves. The "outward" Shanti Nilaya seeks only to help those who are searching and in need to find the "inward" Shanti Nilaya.

FRIENDS OF SHANTI NILAYA

There are now Friends of Shanti Nilaya groups all over the world, started by people who have been touched by our work and who wish now to touch others, people who have worked on their own growth, who have moved toward completion of their unfinished business, and who are in a position to be candles that truly light the way for others.

The purpose of these groups is to support our work and philosophy in their own communities. All activities, programs and services provided by Friends of Shanti Nilaya are free to those who receive them. Those who provide the services are volunteers.

Some Friends of Shanti Nilaya who have received special training are providing screaming rooms in high schools, and some are organizing such rooms in prisons and hospitals. Others offer weekly support groups for recipients to share their painful losses, learn to give up their fears and resolve their guilt. People who come to support groups experience the freedom of confidentiality and unconditional love, without the burden of expectations. Some Friends of Shanti Nilaya are operating sudden-death hotlines for those who have lost a family member or friend through suicide, homicide, accident or unexpected death through illness. Most of these groups provide educational material, knowledge of local resources for the terminally ill and a supportive network for people in their community experiencing pain and crises. All groups sponsor our workshops and lectures.

Whatever the programs, services or activities, Friends of Shanti Nilaya, from the East Coast to the West Coast and in many countries throughout the world, are committed to helping others resolve their unfinished business in the most loving, caring, confidential way in order to live more fully before they die.

One of our most recent moving examples of how Friends of Shanti Nilaya work within our network came when a woman from the Midwest wrote on the bottom of our mail order form in red letters of her helpless, hopeless state of mind. Jane, we will call her, shared her agony and stated she wished to take her own life.

Jane had an unlisted telephone number, which made it impossible for us to reach her immediately. A call was made to Friends of Shanti Nilaya Chicago for assistance. One of the volunteers drove a considerable distance to Jane's house. After a three-hour conversation, Jane made a commitment to live and join the weekly mutual support group sponsored by our Chicago group. We have heard from Jane and already she is working on ideas for helping us lend support to others.

It is wonderful to see the growth of these projects spreading across the world, and I feel blessed to have played a role in their creation and in their nurturing.

4
Betty

❦❧

THROUGHOUT THIS BOOK we will present experiential accounts of our workshops as well as the didactic information necessary to a volume of this kind.

One of the experiences I most often remember is that which we shared with Betty, a middle-aged spinster who lived in the apartment of her sister, a nurse, and her brother-in-law. Betty had a terminal lung disease, looked extremely emaciated and was a picture of skin and bones. She looked far worse than any concentration camp victim I have ever seen.

She showed up at my house one Friday afternoon, barely able to breathe, gasping almost like a fish that was pulled out of the water. With the greatest effort she tried to speak to me, telling me that she drove all the way from her home to my home because she was just ready to explode. And since her energy was so limited she simply could not wait another ten days until I returned from a planned workshop. She was not sure if she would be alive in ten days and had so much pain and unfinished business. She needed to get it off her chest, perhaps even enabling her to breathe somewhat better.

I sat across my coffee table, looking at this woman who seemed to be on her last breath. Gasping for air, she shared a great amount of pain and anguish, of loneliness and rejection, and most of all a tremendous amount of anger and resentment that the only pleasure she had in her life was her faithful boyfriend—and that this boyfriend was barely tolerated in the house of the sister who not only supported her but gave her room and shelter for the final weeks of her life. She wanted to spend every day and every night with her boyfriend, something that was totally unacceptable to the sister, who had very rigid moral rules of behavior and was unwilling to even discuss the matter with her.

I listened to her patiently and with great empathy and wondered why we are so dreadfully judgmental. I wondered why we make it so difficult for many dying patients to get some loving care during the last few days of their lives, when all they need is a hug and a shoulder to lean on. As I often do, I impulsively told her that she just absolutely had to come to my workshop. And that although it was most likely that she might not live to the end of it, every day there in a group of caring, sharing and loving people would be a great blessing. She could leave all her resentment and her hate behind, and even if she died on Tuesday or Wednesday, it would be a positive experience for her to be surrounded by a group of people who would pamper her, love her, sing with her and laugh with her. But most important of all, the group would help her to leave behind all the anguish, the tears, the resentments and the sense of unfairness.

She was most enthusiastic about coming, and it was only after I made this offer that I realized that the workshop was going to be in Colorado Springs. In such an elevated area of the country this woman would probably barely be able to breathe. But following through with my commitment, I called up her physician to ask for permission to "kidnap" her. To my great surprise, and again naturally not by coincidence, he happened to be a pulmonary specialist who had treated me a few years earlier for very severe viral pneumonia. Since he knew me and trusted me, he made me aware of the great risk with this woman's very poor pulmonary capacity, then gave me not only his blessings but also the good advice to get the family's official permission so they wouldn't blame me later on.

Betty went home, confronted her sister and her boyfriend with her plans. Her sister apparently agreed reluctantly, and her boyfriend was delighted that Betty had a chance to spend a few days with caring, loving and open-minded people. The next day he brought her in a wheelchair to O'Hare Airport, where we had oxygen ready. I changed the coach tickets to first-class tickets to give her "the last great treat of her life."

Little did I know that she was afraid of flying and that the window seat I had reserved for her was a threat rather than a pleasure. But with the help of the oxygen and a whiskey sour, she was able to hide her anxiety for the takeoff. When we were over Kansas she was finally able to look out of the window and enjoy the view of the country below.

She attended the whole workshop in a wheelchair. She had a nurse sharing the room with her, listening to her breathing and giving her the necessary medication. In the afternoons, when we took hikes up into the mountains, we secured the van of one of the participants and took her to the highest places on the mountain peaks that we were able to take her by car. From there we carried her to the edge of the mountain, and she enjoyed life very much. She reminded me of a child that had been blind and was able to see for the first time.

Every day she seemed to become younger and healthier. Her breathing became easier as she externalized and shared her agony and pain, her rage and her sense of injustice. She shared with us the few tender moments she had known in her life with her boyfriend, and her great reluctance to return to a home where the presence of her boyfriend was barely tolerated and not really accepted as a loving gift to her life.

On Thursday evening, our last night together, she retired to her room, depressed and unwilling to go back home to Chicago and her sister's home. She started to act out in a typical sulky, moody way, just like a young child who does not want to go to a piano lesson. We did not feed into this negativity but left her alone in her room and told her that we expected her after the breakfast session for our last Friday-morning meeting. She did not show up and none of us went to look for her, as it became clear that she had willed herself to die that morning in order to keep this peak experience as the final day of her life.

We had reminded her of her selfishness and had encouraged her to go home to share the joy with her sister of the growth experience that she had had. We reminded her of the necessity of giving her sister a gift for the care that she had been extended, in spite of the sister's great reluctance and frequent intolerance of the patient's behavior.

At about ten Friday morning, after we had started our morning session without her, we suddenly heard a big crash at the door and an angry wheelchair patient pushed her path through the people into the center of the circle. She reprimanded us for not caring and for not even knowing whether she had died while we had our morning session. We pointed out her negative behavior and acting out, and she was finally able to see how she withdrew and displaced her anger and rage onto other people, something she must have frequently done with her sister. We ended up laughing and hugging each other, and she began to look forward to returning to her home and trying to share some of the positive experiences with her family.

Needless to say, she took home with her a whole telephone booklet full of addresses and telephone numbers. And we gave her a music tape of our singing at the Friday-morning session that she missed. We supplied her for weeks and months afterward with booklets, tapes and musical recordings so she would continue to remember the experience and try to remain positive rather than to use her old negative acting out.

She lived for another year and a half, much to the surprise of the family and the physician. It was less of a surprise perhaps for us, having seen so many critically ill patients emerging out of these workshops with new energy and with a spirit of life that added months and sometimes years to their life span.

5

Emotions as Friends

❧

B E T T Y ' S   S T O R Y dramatically illustrates how, if we have the strength and the courage to confront our own emotions and to accept every one of them as a part of us, we cannot only finish our "unfinished business," but, as we have so often seen, add months and even years to our lives—an observation made over many years, and worth repeating.

We are bombarded daily with our emotions. Some of them are natural; some are not.

What are some of these natural and unnatural emotions? God created man with only five natural emotions, all of which were designed to help him to fulfill his destiny and to experience all the positive experiences that the physical life can offer a human being.

Unfortunately, over the decades and the centuries many of these natural emotions were repressed and replaced with rather unhealthy, destructive or self-destructive emotions, which cause not only much of the turmoil in our own personal lives, but much strain and turmoil in our inter-personal relationships. This leads to power struggles and wars among people and nations, and it has led us on planet Earth close to self-destruction.

Man was created with only two natural *fears*. One of them is of falling, the other one loud noises. Any other fears do not serve to preserve life and are, unfortunately, passed on to children by the grown-ups as a projection of their own fears, their own insecurities, their own ambivalences and sometimes their own anger, revenge and hate. Children who are raised to be afraid of the dark, afraid of man, afraid of crossing the street, afraid to dare and risk, will not develop self-worth and self-love. They will be emotionally crippled, dependent in a clutching, clinging kind of way as well as bitter, resentful and insatiable because no one will ever gratify their needs.

Anger is a natural emotion. The natural form of it requires only fifteen seconds, long enough to say "no thank you," to develop our own inner authority and a healthy assertiveness. Natural anger is never directed at people and is never to be used to harm your fellow man. If you have never been allowed to express natural anger, if you were punished or belted or sent to your room once you expressed a firm and determined "no," you will always have a pool of repressed hate, anger and resentment inside of you, and it takes often a very small spark or trigger to make people explode or to hit somebody or to lash out verbally or physically. Natural anger is handled with understanding and compassion without hurting people physically or emotionally. Natural anger not permitted to be expressed in childhood will develop slowly into hate, revenge and negativity that not only affects our fellow man but affects our health in a more detrimental way than any other negative emotion. Hate literally kills people slowly and gradually unless we are able to let go of it before inevitable physical damage has occurred. We can externalize it and leave it behind. This is a process that has been most rewarding in our workshops where we often find at least one latent mass murderer. When triggered, they will go into a deep homicidal rage for a few minutes. As long as the leaders have no fear of this kind of psychotic homicidal behavior, both the patient and the group are totally safe. The subject who has the courage to share this negativity with his fellow man has to feel totally safe and secure in an environment where he is not only physically protected, but where confidentiality is of the highest order.

Grief is the third natural emotion and serves simply to allow people to come to grips with the thousand little deaths that we experience all throughout our physical existence. The grief for the loss of a security blanket by a child can be as traumatic as the loss of a baby for a mother. For a gardener who acquired a very special tree, to find it dead in the spring or destroyed by vandals can be as devastating as it is for someone to lose a favorite pet. There are a million little deaths as we grow, and each one could be dealt with by the expression of natural grief and tears. We would then be able to move on to new challenges in life. If loss has never been dealt with in an adequate healthy manner as a child, we often become bitter, depressed individuals who drown in our own self-pity and spend most of our time living in the past, regretting the "todays" and worried and fearful about the "tomorrows." Those individuals always feel misunderstood and spend most of their lives looking for others to fulfill their needs—which will never be met. We are responsible for the gratification of our own needs and our own pleasures!

Jealousy is a natural emotion. It helps little children to emulate their friends, to learn to spell, to play the flute, to learn how to ice skate, to read their first book in order to surprise a favorite aunt at Christmas. It is a stimulant for children to achieve, to grow, to learn, to be curious. If this positive jealousy is belittled or punished when we are children, it turns into ugly envy and competition, which has destroyed so many human relationships.

Last but not least, *love* is the most important natural emotion. Very few people in our society really understand and appreciate love. Love consists of two aspects, one of them the holding, loving, cuddling and physical closeness and security. It gives children the feeling that they are beautiful, that they are worth loving, no matter how they look, that they are loved no matter how they behave, and it will assure them of future self-worth and self-respect.

The other aspect of natural love is the ability of a parent to say "no" to a child. There are mothers who tie the shoelaces of their children until they are twelve years old! Needless to say, they cripple their children's self-worth tremendously and will make them always dependent on others. A mother who truly loves will send a child off on the first day of school, no matter how great his anxiety is, and say, "You know, I remember the first day I went to school. I was so proud when I came home and didn't get lost and had an exciting, wonderful day in school. And I bet you can do it just as well as I used to do many, many years ago." A mother who feels confident about her own role as a mother will say to a child, "Honey, I know that you can tie those shoelaces better than I ever did at your age. I will close my eyes and when you have finished, boy, will I be the proudest mother!"

He will learn how to tie his laces and never again ask his mother to do it for him. It is a question of letting go of our own need to do things for others, which is not really an expression of love but an absence of faith that they can do it just as well as any other child.

Sadly, there are many, many children who have never experienced genuine unconditional love. Most of us were raised with "I love you *if* you bring good grades home; I love you *if* you make it through high school; boy, would I love you *if* you went to college, or if I could say one day 'my son, the doctor.' " These children grow up to become prostitutes. They prostitute their minds, they bring awards home, good grades, nice report cards, and they grow up truly believing that you can buy love with good grades, degrees, awards or other worldly kinds of achievements which have nothing to do with love. People who are raised as prostitutes will always look for external verification of their worth. They will always need external approval, they will always be insecure. They may be great achievers and perhaps make it to great societal heights, but they will have very little self-worth and self-esteem. They will spend their life searching for a kind of love that does not exist and never find gratification.

If we could raise one generation of children with unconditional love and firm, consistent discipline (rather than punishment), those people would never have to come to a workshop. They would never have to beat the mattress. They would never have to scream out an ocean of unshed tears. They would not fill society with greed, revenge, hate, envy or self-pity. They would then be able to raise a generation of healthy children who can grow up with harmony between the physical, emotional, spiritual and intellectual quadrants. It is our hope that in our workshops we will be able to teach a few hundred people how to do that, and that they in turn will plant the seeds for new generations, and perhaps in a few generations from now our original planting of seeds will bear fruit and our future children will not live in fear and guilt, unrewarded and ungratified, and ask at the end of their lives, "Is this all there is to living?" Or, "I made a good living, but I never really lived!"

People who are in harmony between the physical, emotional, intellectual and spiritual quadrants become naturally very intuitive. There is no anxiety in their lives and little, if any, stress or turmoil.

They are then best equipped to help others, as there is no unfinished business in their own lives that would cloud their awareness of their own needs as well as the ones of their fellow men. In simple language, "they can live." They will never suffer from a burn-out syndrome and their lives will always be replenished.

NO TWO WORKSHOPS ALIKE

Each workshop somehow has its own dynamics within the already described general structure. No two workshops have ever been alike. As I have mentioned before, every workshop has one or two people present who are special gifts to us; and every workshop has one or two people who do not participate and who leave neutral or negative. These people sometimes become disenchanted or disillusioned, threatened or frightened, because of their own unwillingness or inability to open up and to share.

What makes these workshops very special, however, are the very special events that occur in them. One of these events revolved around a Jewish physician in one of our Sonoma workshops, who virtually became a rabbi at the end of the workshop. A letter written by him about his experiences, in Chapter 15 of this book, will best explain what I mean by a rabbi.

BAPTISM

Another man who had become disillusioned with church teachings spontaneously asked one of the ministers present to baptize him and the whole group of seventy-five people, including agnostics, atheists, Catholics, Protestants, Jews, Hindus and Sufis, joined in a pilgrimagelike walk through the forty acres of Shanti Nilaya toward the natural lake that formed during the rainy season. On a rock at the edge of the water, one of the most moving baptizings took place, reminding almost all of us of John the Baptist in the movie of *Jesus of Nazareth*.

EUCHARIST

We also have photographs of the celebration of the Eucharist at Shanti Nilaya, another very special event that was not planned or scheduled, but simply happened on the spur of the moment. And everyone, regardless of his religious or cultural background, participated and contributed to it.

There is also a prayer that we often use at the end of our workshops: "Thank you, O Spirit of Heaven, for providing us this day."

The significance of this prayer has to do with our conception (and misconception) of what prayers are supposed to do. Most people pray when they want something, and repeatedly say, "give me, give me, give me" and often forget that we are getting all the help that we need, although we very often do not get what we want. We also forget to express thanks for all the blessings, many of which we are unaware of until the time of a crisis when we begin to realize that we are all in good hands. We are not only loved, guided and protected, but also nurtured in many special ways, as every one of these workshops manifests in a thousand ways.

There has never been anyone in these workshops who was not led to be there at the right time, at the right place and with the right people. It is a conglomeration of strangers who meet on Monday and leave as a group of supporting, caring and loving friends on Friday. It makes us aware of what this world could be like if we would share with each other not only our joys but our pain and our sorrows.

When we have finished all the growth work that is possible in so short a time, we usually eat on Thursday evening and then everybody disappears into his own private quarters. Some make themselves very pretty and get dressed up in long dresses or mumus, some in their ritual blue jeans and tops and others suddenly and impulsively do something that they have never done before—such as compose a song or write a poem as the spirit moves them.

Every one of them in his own way contributes something to the fire ritual as we sit around an open fire outdoors, whenever the weather allows. We all share with each other why we thought we were coming to the workshop and what emerged out of this intense sharing in the previous four days. A pine cone thrown into the fire becomes the symbol in which we place all the negativity that we are willing to leave behind and are determined not to take back home with us.

One by one, interrupted only by the singing and the playing of the musical instruments, people step forward and, similar to a public confession, share what aspects of their own personality they are willing to let go.

At the end of this sharing we present one or several loaves of bread, which volunteers from among the participants had baked earlier in the afternoon. And, as the sharing is different and yet the same in each one of the workshops, so are the loaves of bread, whether we have them in Australia, Europe, the United States or Canada. In one workshop, very symbolic of the international character of these retreats, one girl made a Star of David, another one a cross, and a third one made a very special symbol, the ankh, symbol of eternal life.

We break the bread and together with a glass of wine we share in singing and gratitude.

When David, whom you met in Chapter 1, was ready to throw his pine cone into the fire, it was most important that it was his mother who was willing to step forward and hold him up so he could perform this act himself, with the priest who had become his very special friend in between the two of them. It was a moment that Father John will probably never forget. Nor will we forget the sharing, caring love that those people taught everyone who participated in that week.

6

Workshop Purpose

THE WORKSHOPS BEGAN when I realized that, though we were reaching thousands of people every week with the lectures I was presenting, I felt this was not enough. We were not reaching people in a helping way so much as in an informative way. I knew the work that had to be done was larger than this. It had to do more with helping people than telling them about the needs of others. But helping them do what? The answer to me was simple, and came from my years of work with dying patients and their families. The answer was contained in every one of my lectures. People needed help, I told my many audiences, in dealing with their "unfinished business." The workshops were developed as a way of offering that help.

Our goal, our purpose, in these five-day sessions is to help our participants get in touch with their deepest and long-repressed pains, guilt, fears and shame—and thus their unfinished business. We basically teach them what dying patients usually try to do on their deathbed—and that is to finish their unfinished business so they have no more negativity within them and they can literally live until they die with a sense of peace, serenity, acceptance and forgiveness for others and themselves.

It became very clear over these last years, working with healthy people as well as terminally ill patients, that our only enemies are guilt, fear and shame. Such unresolved negativities prevent us from living fully and deplete us of so much energy that even a fight with cancer is a losing battle when we have a sense of punishment, a sense of hopelessness or a feeling of unworthiness to get well. Many of our critically ill patients were able to get in touch with their own self-destructiveness, which had contributed much to the onset of their cancer. They shared their own inner battle or impotent rage, which gradually destroyed them emotionally and physically. They had never felt comfortable enough to share with their fellow human beings who are so often judgmental rather than understanding, who show pity rather than compassion.

In these workshops more and more of our attendees started to share their innermost agonies—stories of incest, of misuse, of being battered children, of unfairness, unfaithfulness, experiences of mistrust and undue punishment as children. These were taboo issues that they never shared with their fellow man before, and that they carried with them as a heavy burden through life. Their traumas often resulted in a specific choice of a profession in a desperate attempt not only to resolve their own agony and pain but to help others in similar situations. It is valid to say that many death and dying specialists go into the field of thanatology because of their own unresolved grief over the loss of a loved one, unconsciously making up with other people what they were not able to do with their own loved ones.

7

Sharing Is the New Beginning

IT IS ONE THING TO SAY 'finish your unfinished business' and another thing to do it. The first question we are always asked is, "Where . . . how . . . do I begin?"

We have found that the beginning comes through sharing. And that is both the *purpose and the method* of our workshops.

It is very clear that we are unable to feel the pain of another human being. The pain of another touches upon the pool of our *own* repressed tears and anguish. It is in the very sharing of the agony of a dying patient that many of our workshop participants are moved to tears; and these tears are the cue for the direction of their own search for their own repressed negativity, which they are later able to become aware of consciously. When they share this with the group, it will again trigger *other* people to share with *their* stories and *their* experiences. In this manner, from Monday night until Wednesday night one triggers another's negativity. The more sharing and the more externalization of pain and agony, the more free and relieved and serene the participants begin to feel. They have an increased sense of great joy, freedom and unconditional love. This is coupled with total forgiveness of their children, or their own grandparents, or their parents, a teacher or a boss, a priest or a minister, a physician or a nurse who hurt them in the past.

They begin to empathize, understanding where those people came from and why they did what they did.

It is important for us to teach the group not to touch others when they are into feelings, as this just puts a "Band-Aid" on their pain, implicitly or explicitly conveying the message: don't cry, it's going to be all right. Our groups very quickly pick up on this and restrain their conditioned response to hug and smooth over painful areas in their neighbor until after the bottled-up tears and rage and anguish have been expressed. It is only after the externalization of the negativity that the group is allowed to hug each other, to touch and console and to pamper each other.

So . . . sharing is the beginning. And through sharing, each participant connects with his own pain, his own repressed grief, his own negativities. And when this connection is made, he is given a safe place and a safe way to externalize that negativity, and get rid of it forever if he chooses to.

How?

It can be done many ways. In our workshops there is really no way—short of physical violence toward another person—that is not allowed. And so one might come to our workshops and hear screaming and wailing, or be confronted by the sight of men and women and young people, too, venting their repressed rage or their sense of unfairness on a mattress, often using a short length of rubber hose we supply.

What is the meaning and the purpose of the beating of the mattress, of the screaming out of the fears, of the shedding of the tears, and noise and wailing in front of a group of from seventy to eighty people, all of whom will be touched by the experience and will begin to realize that they are not the only ones who have a pool of unnatural, unhealthy and energy-draining emotions inside of them? It has been found over the years of work in my Life, Death and Transition

Workshops and in my screaming rooms in hospitals, as well as in other growth groups, that the externalization of negative and unnatural feelings is most therapeutic and that it leaves us with a sense of great relief. Once the bucket of repressed tears, anguish and anger has been emptied, one can correlate and evaluate one's behavior and replace the energy-draining negative behavior with more positive attitudes and responses. Most people react to, rather than act in, life. Most people spend 90 percent of their energy and time worrying about tomorrows and live only 10 percent in the now. Once the pool of repressed negative emotions has been emptied, we can alter those percentages and live a much more full and gratifying and less draining and therefore less ill-health-producing life than before.

This process of active externalization of negativities and repressed emotions became more and more a focal point of the first days of the Life, Death and Transition Workshops. The early workshops contained much verbal sharing. And it was here that I saw a need for a process by which emotions that came to the surface could be experienced, and negativities expelled.

I picked Appleton, Wisconsin, for my first experiment with what I call "active expulsion" (doing something with it), as opposed to "passive discussion" (talking about it). We were again at a Catholic retreat, this time with an incredibly beautiful priest who was in charge of the place and who, in our opinion, was more of a saint than a human being. With his quiet, unconditional love and care he contributed much to the spirit and atmosphere of this beautiful retreat. We were a highly vulnerable group, again with many terminally ill patients with an incredible amount of pain and agony to be externalized, and shared in sometimes very emotional and loud outbursts of rage, hate, anger, agony, screaming and tears. But he was always willing to help his staff to understand what was going on. He functioned as a buffer between those who were used to quiet, meditation and prayer retreats, and those of us who needed a safe place with a professional staff where it was all right to show the most painful and most negative aspects of their being.

We shared so much pain and agony during that week that by Thursday there was nothing this group would not have been willing to share. There was a black woman who attended the workshop who was the picture of pain and agony and quite withdrawn when she came. On Wednesday I took her quietly to a back room where she used a piece of rubber hose, beating the mattress and screaming in agony and pain her physical and emotional starvation as a child. She sobbed out her shame and grief that her mother had to prostitute herself to bring some old cereal home so the children wouldn't starve to death. She shuddered in utter disgust and was close to vomiting when she described how the cereal was full of worms and how her mother forced the children to eat it out of fear that they would starve to death if they wouldn't swallow this repulsive meal.

I pushed this woman to the brink of tolerance when I shoved this imagined food onto her, forced her to eat it and repeatedly hollered at her that she should "be ashamed to reject this food knowing that I sell my body to guarantee that my children are not dying of hunger." The agony, despair, tears, shame and guilt that this woman experienced and shared in this short hour, touched many lives.

While I spend most of my time in the large room with the seventy-five participants, individual participants who either have something most intimate or too lengthy to share are usually taken out by one or two of my assistants into an available adjacent room where they finish up their sharing, go to the deepest depths of their pain and leave it behind. When they return to the main room, they're often beaming and radiant and they have the urge to hug and kiss everybody in their path. They often share the great sense of relief that they have been able to leave their shame and their agony behind, and that they can now proceed with living without carrying these tremendous burdens of guilt and fear and anguish.

It should be said here that in every workshop there are one or two who do not have the courage to break the shell, who sit in the background and watch and observe. They will occasionally perhaps take notes and then disappear before it gets too emotional. Some of them simply close themselves up and leave rather empty, having witnessed a most draining and emotional workshop but not having gained much from it. It became quite evident that those who gained a tremendous amount were those who gave a lot, as it is also in life. The more you give, the more you receive.

One participant tried to figure out all week why in the world she signed up for these five days and was still puzzled about it weeks later. I simply reassured her that there was a significant reason for it which she may only understand months or years later. Five years after her attendance she became the founder of our first hospice for children and pronounced me as the official godmother of the same. Needless to say it is a special blessing to live long enough to see the fruit of our labor, not only on this continent but all over the world.

Another woman was equally puzzled about what literally drove her to California from Canada, when she neither had a dying relative nor any professional involvement in this field. Less than a month after her attendance her son committed suicide and she was grateful for the lessons learned and even more perhaps for the support system, the calls and letters she received from her newly found friends.

Dozens, if not hundreds, of people became involved with the foundings in their areas of "Compassionate Friends" groups, self-support groups of parents who have lost children. The ripple effect is also seen in the hundreds of hospices which sprang up all over the country, although many are not worthy of carrying the name *hospice*. Those that are founded on noble motivation and unconditional love will survive as a beautiful service to the dying; those that get involved in politics, competition and financial motivation as well as prestige will simply not survive.

It is my hope that all hospice personnel will undergo a screening and training that includes one of our five-day workshops.

8

The Process and the Product

As with any friend, we cannot become acquainted with our emotions until we are introduced to them face to face. That is the process of our workshops.

This chapter outlines, in rough form, how things have proceeded in our five-day workshops thus far. All of this is open to change, of course. The workshop is an organic thing, a living thing, and there really is no set format or schedule. Nevertheless, from our earliest efforts to the very latest sessions, we have seen some things in common.

We found, for instance, that the workshop started to follow a certain pattern, not emerging out of any theoretical framework but simply evolving in a natural way. It seemed to gratify the needs of the great variety of people who came to these retreats for a number of different reasons.

ORIGINALLY

The first day was taken up by a rather informal introduction of the participants so that each one had an idea of the diversity of backgrounds and people they were going to live with for the coming week. It also gave the participants a sense of the great number of different reasons for attending a workshop like this. There were people who were in the process of a separation or divorce. There were others pending trial on criminal charges for things they had not done; they had to deal with a tremendous amount of impotent rage and a sense of unfairness and injustice, not knowing where to turn and the end of—and hence the "death" of —their whole way of life . . . and in some cases, their very existence. There were many others who had either the suspicion or the diagnosis of a terminal illness and had to deal with that. There were parents whose children were missing or dying. There was a large number who had lost children under the most traumatic circumstances—sudden, unexpected death, accidents, brutal murder or by long and draining, exhausting terminal illnesses characterized by relapses and remissions, hope and despair. There were also many whose children, parent or sibling had committed suicide.

The introduction brought to the awareness of the group only the most superficial reasons for their coming. Everybody would sit in a circle, often on a pillow on the floor, with elderly, sick or handicapped people on chairs at the outer edge of the circle. The general mood of the group was one of anxiety, caution, fear and a certain skepticism about how in the world we were going to do anything meaningful with such "a big crowd" of people.

The first emotional sharing would occur usually no later than twenty-four hours after their arrival. Most often it happened at the end of the first night, on Monday. Then cancer patients listened patiently to fifty or sixty accounts by loving, caring, beautiful members of the helping professions who, often in poetic and touching language, explained that their reason for being here was simply to be "a better nurse," "a better physician," "a better minister." They sounded so super-caring and loving that all the patients' negative experiences with members of the health professions emerged and they thus "burst the bubble" and destroyed forever the negative images so many of the others in the room had been carrying for years regarding persons in such helping professions.

They would burst into the midst of another "sweet introduction" and start to express their anguish, their disappointments, their rejections, their experiences with people who play games, who don't have the time to listen, who are too busy to care. And before we had finished all the introductions, we were in the midst of experiencing, or at least sharing in, the real-life situations of people who did not get in touch with all the compassion that was presented in the formal introduction.

Once we had had one of these catalysts (which 95 percent of the time was a patient or a bereaved parent), the process continued without any external stimulation or the need for direction, or perhaps even leadership. By Tuesday morning more people were aware of the presence of another fellow human being who shared a similar pain and often, not consciously, they would sit next to each other, encouraging each other. They would share with each other over a cup of coffee, or in silence, some of their mutual experiences and their mutual pain.

By Tuesday morning at the latest, more often on Monday night, I would give every participant a sheet of paper and a box of colored pencils and ask them to draw a picture. I would allow them only ten minutes for its completion to be sure they did it as spontaneously as possible without time to think about how they wanted to present themselves, or to show off what artists they were, or to try to present a picture of love and peace when in fact they felt like a volcano. About a dozen pictures would usually be read and interpreted to show the group that without knowing an individual one can discover an awful lot about that person. And, needless to say, the artists had the free choice to share then as much as they were ready to share in front of the group about the validity of the interpretation and to elaborate on the details of the conflict that became manifest in their pictures.

Susan Bach, a London Jungian psychoanalyst, started to use this technique in a hospital in Zurich, where I had worked for over a decade beginning in the fifties. Together with Mr. Weber, an artist who worked extensively with children who had brain tumors, she discovered that the patients' spontaneous drawings revealed their awareness of their illness, progress or regression even when they were too young to understand their predicament intellectually.

In an out-of-print publication, "Spontaneous Paintings of Severely Ill Patients," they described their findings as well as their technique to elicit this preconscious material. We are using this method almost daily as an easy and reliable as well as always available and inexpensive tool to screen people and to give us a clue about the seriousness of a person's often hidden and deep-seated problems.

It was during those first years of my one-week workshops that my work began to shift from working with dying adults to working almost exclusively with dying children. I developed an increased interest and understanding of the depths of knowledge, wisdom and communication of dying children. I became more and more involved with Susan Bach's method of using spontaneous pictures by children to know "where they were at." Her interpretations of drawings by terminally ill patients had a great influence on my work and have contributed more to my understanding of the psyche of terminally ill children than probably any other single publication.

It became increasingly clear that the spontaneous pictures made by these children, as well as by adults, would reveal the same material as the dreams of these patients. Their pictures reveal not just their conscious knowledge of their impending death, but also their preconscious awareness of their destiny. Also shown are their hidden pains and conflicts and their often deep-seated anxieties.

Working with many, many terminally ill patients across the country, usually between flights or between lectures, gives me very little time to evaluate the specific needs of my out-of-town patients. The use of this tool allows me within a few minutes to get to the bottom of their pain, anxieties and awareness without the need of long time-consuming psychiatric evaluation and case histories.

I have worked with hundreds of dying children and never found one case in which this method did not reveal much meaningful material—material that would help me to help them in a very short time and get to the essence of their conflicts. I saw no reason why this method could not be applied to "healthy people" and so I used my workshops again to experiment, to see if much of this understanding that comes through this method of interpretation of spontaneous drawings could be used by counselors and ministers.* It could become a tool to cut through the layers of defensiveness that require so many hours of therapy before any effective changes can take place.

---

* The basic premise of the interpretation of drawings is described in Susan Bach's paper as well as in *Living with Death and Dying* (New York: Macmillan Publishing Co., Inc., 1981), by Elisabeth Kübler-Ross. Additional bibliography on art interpretation is as follows: Bach, Susan. *Spontaneous Paintings of Severely Ill Patients.* Printed in Germany, 1969 Buswell, Guy Thomas. *How People Look at Pictures.* Chicago: University of Chicago Press, 1935. Danz, Louis. *The Psychologist Looks at Art.* New York: Longmans, Green & Co., 1937. Ehrenzweig, Anton. *The Psycho-Analysis of Artistic Vision and Hearing.* New York: Julian Press, Inc., 1953. Grant, Jr., Niels. *Art and the Delinquent.* New York: Exposition Press, 1958. Guggenheimer, Richard. *Sight and Insight.* New York: Harper & Brothers Publishers, 1945. Jakab, Irene, ed. *Art Interpretation and Art Therapy.* New York: S. Karger, 1952. Kris, Ernst. *Psychoanalytic Explorations in Art.* New York: International Universities Press, Inc., 1952. Whittaker, James K., and Trieschman, Albert E., eds. *Children Away from Home.* New York: Aldine Publishers, 1972.

The process worked wonderfully in the workshops. It was a very moving experience for me to see how many people in less than twenty-four hours of togetherness are willing to bare their souls, to elaborate on the pain that was reflected in their pictures and to confirm some of the more deep-seated, real reasons for their coming to a workshop.

Many of the people who have been most impressed by our "reading" of their pictures at the beginning of the workshop, and especially those who make incredible strides and progress during the week, give us as a gift another spontaneous picture at the end of the week which clearly shows the tremendous growth that occurs in such an extremely short time.

9

The Rules

I NEED NOT SAY that there have to be some strict rules of behavior when seventy to eighty people from all backgrounds spend a week together in sharing and experiencing the joys and pains of life. Confidentiality is an absolute must, and no tape recording is permitted during the session, except for the times of didactic teaching.

There are two important points that I want to mention. The first has to do with the introductions at the beginning of the workshop, where we all use first names. There are many people coming to these workshops who have heard me previously at lectures or at honorary degree ceremonies who put me on a pedestal or try to make a guru of me. One way of coping with this worship aspect is to stop all formalities. So we make a rule on that first day that anybody who calls me Dr. Ross has to pay ten dollars in cash instantly, and anybody who calls me Dr. Kübler-Ross pays twenty-five dollars. Since most people are not financially well-to-do, this stops them from using it. The moment they begin to make a slip, somebody gives them a friendly kick so that by the first evening they get into the habit of calling me Elisabeth. We jokingly say that this money is used to buy the wine for the ritual on the last evening. (It is always understood that during the workshops no drugs or alcohol are permissible, except for the ritual wine on Thursday evening.) We have never received more than ten dollars in any given workshop, and it breaks the ice right from the beginning.

The second aspect is that even though some people live in close proximity to the workshop site, commuting is not permissible. This is partially because we work often late into the night. But it is also because we want to become one intensely sharing community. If people left, it would split the group up into those who commuted and those who stayed together.

We also discourage relatives, mates and people with a close work relationship from attending the same workshop. We always place them in different workshops in order to enhance their own personal growth work without inhibition and mutual protection. Since each workshop is very different and yet very similar, they have the advantage that they can both come home and share their own individual experiences without being inhibited by a co-worker, a mate, a mother or a daughter. Sharing some of the negative experiences is much simpler to do among strangers than among relatives! Parents who are in the process of losing a child, or share a common tragedy, are, naturally, exceptions to this rule.

Many people who attend these workshops have been on tranquilizers, especially Valium, for months and years. This has most often been prescribed for them at a time of crisis. After the crisis they are often not advised to discontinue their use, but rather encouraged to continue to take these drugs. It is our encouragement that allows most of these people to wean themselves from all tranquilizers, pep-up pills and/or sleeping pills. By the end of the workshop there are indeed very few who take drugs, with a few exceptions of diabetics, epileptics and cardiac patients who, naturally, need some maintenance medications.

We always have meals together. We work in the morning

and then give the group two hours off either to sleep, rest or write in their diaries or logbooks, to give them an opportunity to evaluate and correlate their experiences. While writing down their thoughts and feelings they often gain a tremendous amount of insight into their behavior and their reactions. We also offer a meditation teacher who makes himself available during the early afternoon to teach those who are interested some relaxation techniques and meditation in order to add a different and additional dimension to their lives.

At 4:00 P.M. we resume our work again until dinner, followed by an evening session which lasts until any time between 10:00 P.M. and three in the morning. The time is always dependent on the most vulnerable in the group, namely our terminally ill patients, who begin to get sleepy and can no longer be receptive or participate. We usually break up the whole group so that those who are weak, sick or tired do not miss any opportunity of participation.

While the relaxation and meditation sessions are usually held outdoors, the actual sharing and growth work has to be done indoors, because of the usually quite emotional and noisy sharing of pain and agony, accompanied often by screaming and beating of a mattress to express in a physical way the pain and the anguish. Since we are all rather close together in one room, it is impossible to be distracted by a group of flying birds, by butterflies in the bushes or by the many dogs who like to visit. Since we are in crowded quarters and many people are allergic or oversensitive to smokers, we have what we call our "physiologic break" every hour and a half to two hours. Then we stretch our legs, have a cup of tea or coffee or a cigarette; others simply take a breath of fresh air and sunshine before we resume our work again.

10

The Significance of Music

❧

ALL WORKSHOP PARTICIPANTS are asked to bring musical instruments, such as flutes, recorders, guitars and cymbals. Those who don't play usually bring some book, teaching tapes or other significant teaching materials, so that each one contributes a gift in his or her own way to the fullness of the week. As the old American Indians used to chant, as the Benedictine monks started their famous choirs, as the monks of the Western Priory in Vermont express their love for God and man and life in music, as all religious services all over the world have learned to enhance their moments with singing and music, so we have learned that the singing of people together enhances the present energy a hundredfold. We begin every session with singing, and we not only work hard, but share joy, pride and happy moments, such as when we sing and dance around the Thursday night bonfire. Many elderly men and women (we have had many in their 80s and 90s and one over 100 years old) who have not used their singing voices in decades have started to sing again with us.

Instead of being awakened by a harsh bell, almost every workshop has a volunteer who wakes us up with beautiful flute music, which makes it impossible to start the day in a bad mood.

RESOLUTION—THURSDAY-NIGHT RITUAL

All these issues come to light in these intense and most emotional workshops. They are shared together and are externalized until the person is willing not only to forgive others but to forgive himself. The sense of joy, relief and pride that follows cannot be described in words but has to be witnessed, especially during our most meaningful Thursday-night ritual. At that time the participants are asked to place their pain, agony, guilt, grief, fear and shame symbolically into a pine cone and then one after the other steps forward and throws the pine cone into the fire. They share for the last time with the group what they are willing to leave behind and not take back home with them to interfere with their fullness of life.

11

Participants

❦

WHEN PEOPLE HEAR OF OUR WORKSHOPS, we quickly receive what has now become a very common inquiry: how do you choose participants? Can anyone attend? Must one be terminally ill? et cetera.

The selection of workshop participants is very simple. When we receive requests from interested persons to attend one of our workshops, we put them on the waiting list and send them a registration form asking for some very basic information. We are not interested in knowing their academic background or professional standing. We simply need their name, address and telephone number, and their basic motivation to attend one of these workshops. We need to know whether they are terminally ill and cannot wait for a year, whether they are old and need special attention—namely the ones who are seventy, eighty and ninety years old, so that we have some special sleeping accommodations for them rather than sleeping bags or bunk beds. We naturally give preferred treatment to anyone with a terminal illness, to people with colostomies or who need special nursing care. For these people we assign a nurse-roommate to give medical and nursing attention during the five days.

Those who have just lost a child through murder, accident, suicide or illness will never be put on a waiting list. We believe strongly that the sooner they can deal with the loss and the pain, the sooner they can start living again. We developed the policy that anybody over eighty, anybody with a potentially terminal illness and anybody who is losing or has just lost a loved one does not go on the long waiting list but gets the next conceivable opening in any workshop in the country where they are physically able to attend.

We also experimented with people in extremely vulnerable physical conditions—people two weeks prior to their actual physical death, quadriplegics who need to be attended around the clock—and have found that rather than being a problem these people give us more joy and growth experiences than perhaps any other workshop participants. For every multiple sclerosis patient, we get three more referrals of multiple sclerosis patients and have developed quite an expertise working with them. We have learned to work with these patients, as well as patients rendered quadriplegic as a result of accidents, to help them to share, and to assist them in externalizing their pain, their anger and their anguish. This they are able to do in spite of the fact that they cannot use their arms or legs to express their rage. (Later on we will describe some of these experiences with these very special people who always have been a gift to our workshops.)

Now we regularly take quadriplegics, accident victims, Vietnam victims and people who exist in VA hospitals and nursing homes looking out of the window, literally unable to move a finger, an arm or a leg, totally dependent on the care of others. We are grateful for the participants of previous workshops who "have been there" and have grown. They return a year, or two, or three years later on "to recharge their batteries," and by their own sharing, their own example of their own inner strength, courage, honesty and growth give the impetus to those who are just starting their own growth work.

Many of the people who come to our workshops expecting

to hear great academic, intellectual, didactic material start Monday with notepads on their knees, pen in hand, or with a tape recorder, and are at first deeply disappointed that they have to watch the tears, the screaming and the agony of their fellow man. If they are incapable of watching the pain of their fellow man, they are naturally never going to be good teachers. They cannot teach others how to listen to the pain and the anguish of a dying patient without being drawn into the pool of their tears and their anguish. It is those professionals that later on need psychiatric help, that later on have to change their careers, that later on are "burned out," or develop ulcers, high blood pressure and coronaries. The stress of their work and the listening to this agony day in and day out have resulted in psychiatrists' having the highest rate of suicide among professionals in the United States.

Many counselors and therapists come to these workshops trying to "compare notes" with their school of thinking and their method. They try for several days to criticize the crudeness and simplicity of our method. But they are stunned by Friday when they see that seventy-five strangers have become a sharing, loving group of people who have been willing to share the deepest depth of their souls with their fellow man. They see these people emerge with a sense of purification, freedom and a sense of great relief that they had never experienced before.

Many of the participants have been in psychiatric treatment or counseling. Many professionals have gone through years and years of psychoanalysis. And yet the depth of experiences that emerge in these workshops is tenfold what one would experience after five or six years of daily analysis. I have experienced this myself and have reached memories and repressed pain that never emerged during the most classical and, to me, very gratifying psychoanalysis.

I point this out not to criticize psychoanalysis, but to

compare the meaningful and lasting benefits of this form of group process. It produces an awareness that is solely due to the courage, the honesty and the willingness of strangers to bare their souls and to share their pain, thus giving a gift to seventy-five fellow participants by touching their own pool of pain and giving them the choice to share it and leave it behind. Each one who shared gave a gift to seventy-five others, and they in turn shared their pain; so that by the middle of the week every participant had experienced hundreds of traumas, many of which touched their own memory bank and their own pool of repressed negativity. It is impossible to sit through this workshop as an observer and note taker without being touched by the humanity of a mixed and beautiful group of courageous, loving and honest people.

Finally, regarding participants, I want to make the observation that as each workshop began it became very clear to me that the people who were there were not there by coincidence, but that we always had the "right kind of group." I mean by this that even the proportion of health professionals and patients seemed to be ideal, as well as the proportion of male to female, young and old, as well as lay people and professionals. In the same workshop we very often had a hospital administrator or a medical director of a big corporation, as well as a nurse's aide, patients, hospital chaplains, lay people and housewives, an electrician from New York City, a philosopher from northern California or a yoga teacher or "guru" who in other workshops would normally be adored and put on a pedestal. In our group everyone was just one of the family.

Many well-known people have attended these workshops. Since it is a rule for participation that we only call each other by the first name, very few people were aware when we had a famous participant among us. Sometimes on the very last day when we were rid of our hangups and our prejudices, I would make a private joke out of introducing our "formal guests" to the group at a time when they had already had a chance to get to know them as human beings and not as celebrities.

One of the most rewarding adventures of this kind was the attendance by Ram Dass, who came to one of my workshops in Colorado Springs. At the time he was probably at the peak of his fame and followed by thousands of worshipers who treated him more as a god than as a human being. We had made a private arrangement that he would come to participate in my workshop under one condition —that he came as a human being and not as the famous guru of thousands of youngsters in a time of great upheaval among our college campuses. He promised to abide by this rule.

Until he showed up on the retreat place, I was not sure that he would actually honor me with his presence, and I was most delighted when he appeared. Although dressed in an unusual attire, he nevertheless remained rather anonymous for the first three days. Many elderly ladies who had never heard of Ram Dass, abiding by the rules of the workshop, called him Ram, which means god. And I couldn't help discovering a light chuckle in his face, not being used to being an anonymous Mr. Ram. Later on when the group had become a true, genuine family, we finally officially introduced him and he gave one of the most moving evening sessions about his own work with the issue of death and dying, especially his work with prisoners on death row.

His and my work shed a light into the vital issue of this whole concept of dealing with life and death. The most important aspect of it perhaps is that the awareness of possible and imminent death brings about either the very best in people or the very worst. It became clear to both Ram Dass and myself, in our involvement with people in this kind of predicament, that the awareness of a very limited life span "in the midst of life" changes the total values of men and women and makes them reevaluate their own existence. It puts them in touch with a spiritual dimension, which is more often than not totally obliterated during our busy life-style pursuing of "fortune and happiness." It was after the death penalty was commuted to a life sentence that almost every single prisoner resumed certain negative behaviors and very quickly lost that spiritual aspect that made them so very special during the weeks they were waiting to be called to the electric chair.

In every single workshop we have had in the last ten years, we always had one special guest like Ram Dass. This was an attempt on my part to bring new dimensions into every workshop and to shed light on areas that are often forgotten. Many of the people who have attended these workshops work in the community with delinquents, with first offenders, or in the penal system of this country which leaves so much to be desired and which is in such desperate need for rejuvenation, for a new approach to help people rather than to punish them.

We have many special plans for the future to help change this country's penal system using the approach that we have employed now for a decade in our workshops. At first these workshops were used mainly to help dying patients and their families. Later on they also helped the health professionals as well as lay people to live more fully. Ultimately they will help those people who have gone on a path of crime because of their own pain and anguish and unfinished business, something that is very preventable if they experience understanding rather than judgment.

As a special treat to the workshop participants, I at one time invited Dr. and Mrs. Carl Simonton to attend one of our retreats. Dr. Simonton co-authored the best-seller *Getting Well Again,* which has revolutionized the treatment of patients with serious illness—particularly cancer—by suggesting that cures can be effected through visualization. His lovely wife has worked closely with him in his work and in giving seminars, lectures and programs throughout the country on the visualization technique. At another occasion I invited Rev. Dr. Mwalimu Imara, a beautiful Gestalt therapist and old friend of mine who was the only minister who stuck it out with me fifteen years previously at the University of Chicago when everybody else deserted the ship because of the resistance and hostility of the staff, who did not want the dying patients to be interviewed.

At almost every workshop a special person showed up, one that I never chose, that I was never aware of ahead of time. One was always present and turned out to be the blessing and the special personal gift to me.

One of these people was a Zen master in Hawaii who, in his introduction, calmly and with great serenity said, "I don't know why I'm here." I blurted out, "You are a gift to me." Not surprised, he quietly added, "That is quite possible." And was he *ever* a gift to me!

Mitz, as we all called him, came from a long, beautiful background of training, with an understanding of Zen Buddhism and with an ability to share and to talk in a way that I had never heard before. He used beautiful parables, often not understood by many of the participants until the next day, when they had enough time for contemplation and evaluation and then became aware of the beauty of his communications.

It was in the same workshop that we invited a mother of a three-year-old child. She had called on very short notice to tell us that she was unable to participate because she was not able to find a baby-sitter for her dying little child. Her youngster was the size of a six-month-old baby, unable to sit or talk or function in any way beyond a newborn baby. Again rather impulsively, I told her to simply bring her baby along and we would somehow make arrangements,

Elisabeth Kübler-Ross with David

David's mother and father with Elisabeth Kübler-Ross at
Shanti Nilaya

David and his mother at the workshop

David and friends in the
pool

David and his mother

David at the fire

"It was important for us to teach the group not to touch others when they were in feelings."

Beating the mattress

Linda with Lois (David's mother) at Shanti Nilaya

One special moment was Jamie's sixth birthday

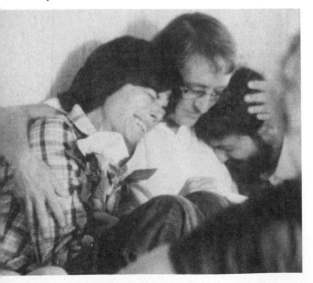

Linda, Jamie, and Elisabeth Kübler-Ross

Lee made a beautiful stained glass butterfly for Linda

Linda with Rob, who had also lost a child

"Rob became aware that he was not alone having pain."

Rob submerged himself in the pool and was then able to open so
of the thoughts and feelings he needed to share.

Paul

The only thing I wanted to do was to hug you."

ıl: "Hey, here I am and I
e you!"

"I'd come here with a broken heart and that's
what I was leaving behind."

Geri being fed at the workshop

Geri dictating her drawing

Geri and Elisabeth Kübler-Ross at the workshop

Geri: "It made me unafraid."

Tanya

Elisabeth Kübler-Ross holding up Tanya's drawing

"I feel deprived."

"I feel less than half alive."

Tanya singing Russian songs

Tanya on the last day of the
workshop

Elisabeth Kübler-Ross

that we could all contribute to the care of this critically ill child, who had so many malformations that it was not expected to live.

When she arrived with her three-year-old child, we arranged for a hanging swing that he could put his feet into and swing from the ceiling. We hung it in the midst of the workshop conference room and watched this little baby virtually exist as a vegetable. He was not able to focus his sight on any object, was not able to cry or smile or even swallow. He was fed every few hours through a little tube.

By the middle of the week we suddenly began to recognize changes in this little child. He began to look at people. He began to react and behave differently when we started to sing. And by the end of the week he actually focused on the participants and managed his first smile.

No one, including his physician, expected him to live beyond this week. Kimo died two and a half years after the workshop. His mother has had time to come to grips with many of the problems that she was able to share with a listening group of caring people who all fell in love with her little boy, who had been willing to pitch in at the times when she needed to get a break in the twenty-four-hour care of this totally dependent infant.

It is people like Kimo and Betty and many of our quadriplegic friends, who—although they have great problems —have been the greatest contributors in our workshops, helping participants to develop a sense of compassion and an understanding of human behavior. They go beyond the common narrow-minded, judgmental, and so often punitive and arrogant attitudes toward others.

12
The Loss of a Child

❧❧

LINDA, LEE AND ROB

MANY OF THE WORKSHOP PARTICIPANTS
come, not to prepare for a death in the family or for their
own impending death, but because I had previously taken
care of a dying family member or child. Sometimes, after
the funeral is over and the family settles down to the old
"routine," the parents are willing to join us to resolve whatever grief or unfinished business they have left.

One of these people was Linda, whose story is already
described in the book *To Live Until We Say Goodbye*, who
lost her little Jamie to a brain tumor.

Linda came accompanied by the male nurse at the Babies'
Hospital in New York who took such special, loving care
of Jamie during the last few weeks and months of her life.
We encouraged both of them to come together as they had
shared the depths of despair and also the joy in Jamie's
death. It was mainly due to Lee's willingness to be available
that Linda had the courage to take Jamie home to die.

They arrived the morning of the workshop and although
still bereaved, they naturally felt secure and safe in each
other's presence. Mal Warshaw and I were also familiar
faces who had shared the final months of Jamie's life with
them, and they felt comfortable and at home at Shanti
Nilaya.

The mother's main purpose was to come to grips with the grief over the loss of her only little girl, and also to gain some understanding into the behavior of the surviving brother, Rusty. He had acted out off and on prior to the death of his sister, and naturally had some feelings when the mother left him again for a week to go to California to attend the workshop.

Lee's main interest was to see how staff can be trained to become more sensitive to and aware of the needs of dying children and the families that he took care of.

Linda came not only for herself, to resolve her own grief and sense of loss over her little girl, but to share her experiences with the group. And now, through her sharing in the book, she is also sharing them with the world as an example of what it is like when we do everything we can. She shows how when we honestly and openly share our pain, our grief, our tears and our joys, we can lose a beloved child without any grief work to do, but with simply the natural grief that will resolve in time without all the guilt and the shame and the fear that result from feeling that we have not done everything we can possibly do.

It was her participation that affected so many lives and brought many parents in touch with their own shame, their own guilt, their own remorse, for their lack of openness or lack of courage in similar situations. And a physician who was present at the workshop questioned Linda and Lee about how to deal with parents of terminally ill children, then returned to his own practice with an incredible learning experience that will benefit so many of his patients and their families.

One of the shortcomings of these very intense five-day workshops is that we usually sit in a crowded place on pillows on the floor. We get so involved that we forget our muscles and that the body also needs exercise. So during every physiological break there may be somebody who is good in leading calisthenics, others who go jogging around for a little while and yet others, like Lee and Linda, who go for a stroll through the meadows, sharing, touching, remembering, crying and laughing together, feeling as close as a brother and sister who haven't seen each other for a while.

JAMIE'S BIRTHDAY

There are always very special moments in these workshops, and one of these special moments was Jamie's sixth birthday, a few months after her death. Since we all remembered the date, we tried to make a very special event out of it and we surprised Linda by singing Jamie's favorite songs. I went out into the yard and picked some flowers from the Shanti Nilaya garden and gave them to Linda to mark that special occasion. Needless to say, the beautiful lily touched Linda's heart and she sobbed tears of sadness over the death of her little girl. She sobbed for her inability to have Jamie with her, to bake a birthday cake for her, to see her blow out the candles and to see her happily open up packages or chase balloons. Lee made a beautiful stained glass butterfly for Linda for this special day; the butterfly symbolizes Jamie's present state after she has shed her physical body, which we call, symbolically, the cocoon.

It was the butterfly and the flowers, the sharing and the remembering, rather than an attempt to cover up this painful day, that helped Linda to emerge out of it smiling and with new courage to spend her first year of the death of her little girl surrounded by friends and supporters rather than denying the reality of it and carrying the pain through the rest of her physical life.

Built into the workshops are also times for reflection and solitude. Those who are not interested in attending meditation or relaxation techniques simply go up into the mountains, sit on a rock, listen to some flute or guitar playing. Some sit under a tree and meditate in their own way without ever having taken any classes and simply listen to the sounds of nature, of the grass whispering in the wind, the butterflies that fly around all over the place and the singing of the birds.

ROB

It was in a quiet moment like this that Rob and Linda met at the workshop. Rob also had lost a child and he did not get much support anywhere. He arrived at the workshop with a tremendous amount of pain and anger, on the verge of leaving his pregnant wife and starting a new life on his own. I had met them only once before at my house where they had asked for a consultation. I had felt a strong urge to take him on the spur of the moment, as usual, to my workshop. I felt that his wife was in a better place at the present, but that he needed to get in touch with his anger and rage so that he would not displace it onto his wife and leave her with the unborn baby in a crucial time like this.

It was Linda's experience with Jamie, their sharing, and his willingness to listen to the tremendous pain of others that made him aware that he, although going through a painful loss, had been spared the tremendous drain of a long-lasting, depleting and costly terminal illness, which would have probably brought him not only to the brink of financial disaster but also to the end of his reserve energy and strength.

He lost his little child quickly and suddenly by drowning. He had no time for any preparatory grief, or going through any of the stages of dying described in my earlier books. He had dropped the denial of the reality of the death of his child and just went through a tremendous amount of rage and anger. When he came to the workshop, he was asking why this had to happen to him. And it was through the externalization of his rage and anger, of the sense of unfairness, and by listening to all the tremendous amount of pain and agony that seventy-five people shared willingly and voluntarily with him that he became aware that he was not alone in his pain.

It was toward the very end of the workshop that he ran out of the workshop room toward the pool. I followed him quietly, not knowing what he was up to. I simply watched him from a distance as he jumped into the pool, which is in the garden of Shanti Nilaya. One of his fears that he shared earlier was ever getting near water.

It was after he was finally able to pour out his pain and his grief and his tears that he ran off and, fully dressed, with one big jump went and submerged himself in the pool. Until the workshop he had been unable to enjoy his two favorite avocations, music and swimming. I silently sat at the edge of the pool, let him swim under and above the water, waiting for him to come out and willing to listen if he chose to share. After a few minutes of wild swimming back and forth, he swam toward me, simply hanging over the edge of the pool, touching my feet, thinking, evaluating, correlating and then finally opening up some of the thoughts and the feelings that he needed to share.

It was a most moving experience for me, knowing that this young father would return home to his wife. I knew he was truly looking forward to the new baby and would be able to resume his music and swimming, to share this with his family.

PAUL AND CHERYL

I met Paul and Cheryl at the airport in San Francisco when I was returning hoarse and quite tired and exhausted from three days of lecturing on the northern coast of California. I was just ready to get my boarding pass when a young couple approached me with the request to have a few minutes to talk to me. I had been surrounded by needy and desperate people for the preceding three days, and I felt depleted of resources and energy.

I took one look at this bearded, huge man who would have looked like a Santa Claus had it not been for his reddish hair and his terribly sad face, which appeared to be in a sort of shock and numbness. It was Cheryl, his young wife, who started to talk. While I received my boarding pass, they revealed in a few sentences that their only son had died a few weeks before of aplastic anemia at the age of nine years. And then a week and a half after his funeral, their eleven-year-old daughter was rediagnosed as being full of cancer. They needed help, and they needed it desperately.

I looked at my watch and looked at the waiting crowd ready to board the plane, and I said in my usual, quiet prayer, "God, give me one hour to talk to these people. That's probably all I would need." And just as I was in the process of answering Cheryl, telling her that my plane was ready to board, a loudspeaker sounded with an impressive voice right over our heads, "Flight number 83 will be delayed by one hour." I said my silent, "Thank you, O Spirit of Heaven, for providing me this chance." And we ended up sitting in the gate area of Flight 83 to San Diego. We talked for an hour about the pain, the numbness, the agony and the despair that they experienced.

What else could I do but tell them about our research in death and in life after death. I told them of the need to communicate with their eleven-year-old daughter and not allow their numbness and pain to interfere with the perhaps short time they had with their only surviving child. I asked them to come as my guests to the next workshop, which was at Oceanside, knowing that if both parents could leave their dying girl for five days the rewards would be great for the parents and their child.

And so they came, and they not only contributed an incredible amount of wisdom and learning to a group of eighty people, but they left the workshop being themselves changed and transformed, open and loving again. It is presumptuous of me to try to share what happened within those two lovely people. And so I asked Paul and Cheryl to tape record in their own words what they had experienced during these five short but transforming days.

PAUL

Hello, Elisabeth, this is Paul. First I want to send you my love and the hope that things are going well for you. You had told Cheryl you wanted our feelings on the workshop, before, during and afterwards. So I'll just get right into it.

Before coming to the workshop my life had really been one of stress and tension, my son having been dead only a few months and then my daughter, Kamala, being rediagnosed with osteosarcoma. I was really at a point in my life where there was nothing meaningful. I felt very empty.

Having heard of your work and having read some of the things that you had written on the subject of death and dying, I knew I wanted at some point to make contact with you. Also, I'd heard one of your tapes and something in me made a connection with you, through the sound of your voice. So any kind of hesitations or reservations I may have had about expressing myself in a strange situation were put aside, and I wanted this experience. And so, we came.

Once at the workshop my first reaction was that this is not really what I had expected. This is not what I was looking for, this is not what I thought was going to happen, this is not the kind of information I thought I needed. I wasn't sure. I was really kind of confused at first, watching other folks scream and holler and making what I thought to be kind of a show of it at first. I really didn't see myself as being able to participate in that kind of experience in front of so many people. And so for the first few days I just viewed it as sort of an emotional circus, you know. It just didn't seem like I could get anything out of it. So I just continued to hold onto my considerations about who I was and what I should be doing about what was happening in my life with the death of my son and the illness of my daughter.

By midweek I began to see the value of it, and I wanted to do it very much. I saw people going down to the mat and beating and screaming, getting this kind of release. I knew on some level that here was something I could use in myself if I would allow myself that experience. Letting it go, in front of a group like that, sharing, I knew I would feel differently. But because of who I am, or who I think I am, I felt I needed to hold onto a lot, to maintain a certain dignity, a certain kind of social bullshit. And I continued with that consideration for the first few days.

About the third or fourth day at breakfast you caught me and mentioned that maybe your assistant could help me. We could go off in another room and do it that way. And that sort of rang a bell for me. I said okay. I was ready for that because before you mentioned that I was really ready to leave. It was just becoming more than I could deal with.

So when he took me out and took me into the room, he didn't really have to do much. I was ready. It was really ready to come, and I guess I just needed the privacy for that to happen. Because once we got into the room, it happened. I just let it go and started crying and screaming and yelling and pounding the mattress. It just came, and it continued to come in what seemed to be torrents. Once I allowed that to happen, it seemed like there was no stopping, there was no ending. And the more I got into it, the better it felt; even though on one level I was still sort of observing myself, looking in on this situation, you know, on another level it was much more significant. And it just continued to come out. The tears flowed and my nose ran and your helper was there with the tissues and the encouragement and the support and the guidance to keep me in that form. And the more I got into it the more —I'm kind of at a loss for words here—it just continued to go on and on.

And then as I was on my knees, rocking back and forth and sobbing, thinking about my son and my daughter and then my life, I realized that I wanted to let go of all the pain and all the heartache and the incredible anguish. I found myself saying, "I give up. I don't want to fight this anymore. I give up. I surrender. I surrender." And as I continued to repeat those words, "I surrender, I give up," I felt myself as a little baby. I felt myself becoming smaller and smaller and smaller, on a level that I didn't quite understand. And the words continued to form in my mind and come out, "I give up, I surrender." The only thing I could latch onto, or feel comfortable with, was "God help me."

When that came out I seemed to literally lift off the mat. Just a couple of inches, just enough to let me know that something incredible had just happened. And I felt a sort of numbness, and your assistant came and touched me and asked if I would come and share this with the group. He had to help me off the mattress because I literally couldn't stand up on my own. So he supported me and walked me out into the hallway and back into the lounge, to the conference room, and sat me down in front of a chair.

As I was sitting there, there was a lady on the mattress sharing, so there was a bit of a delay. As I sat there, the feeling that I had, the only thing that I could think about was this yogi expression of being "blissed out." I just felt this incredible bliss.

And so when you asked me to share that with the group, I looked at all the faces, and looked around me. I didn't know what to say because it had been on a level I had never experienced. I've taken a few drugs where I've had experiences of that nature, but this was much more . . . *organic* is the word I come up with. I'm not sure if that expresses it; but on drug experiences, the feeling was of a drug experience. In this experience, in this situation, in this way of seeing myself, it was on a much deeper level. By deeper I mean that it wasn't in my head, it was in my guts. And I was numb and tingly and just sort of bursting with something I had never quite experienced before.

And when you asked me again to look up at the group and tell them what had happened, I looked around the group until I saw Cheryl's face, and that was like an anchor point for me. I knew

I could do it, but what I could do was not to verbally say, "Hey, this is what happened." But I could look at the group and say, "Hey, here I am, and I love you." And I looked over at you and realized how true that was, because the only thing I wanted to do with you was to hug you and be close to you. And that's what happened, you came and put your arms around me and I recall again just bursting into tears. Not tears so much of happiness or joy so much as just realizing that, hey, this really was me. I'm real to myself, you know?

My fears and my anxieties and my heartbreak were there, but they didn't have the mass or the significance I had once felt them to have. I was overwhelmed. I was overwhelmed by my own sense of serenity in this kind of situation, in front of all these people. Because I knew they loved me as much as I loved them. I really saw the value of sharing. I've never shared on that level before. Maybe, not even . . . maybe with one or two people in my whole life. And then it wasn't really clear, and then I felt kind of embarrassed. But in this situation there was no embarrassment, no hesitation or anything like that. It was just pure, from the heart. It was really from my heart, and it was just kind of wonderful.

And then I went out and went to lunch, and lunch was just sort of a wonderful little interlude. Then, coming back, sitting on the grass with Cheryl and sharing with her what I was feeling, my heart opened up in such a way as it had never opened up to her before. And she felt that in me. We were just ecstatic with each other, on a nonverbal kind of level.

And then that night at the bonfire, thinking what it was that I had come to the workshop for and what I had experienced and what I was willing to give up, it all became very crystal clear. I'd come there with a broken heart, and that's what I was leaving behind. It was so simply beautiful that I was almost patting myself on the back. I almost had a swelled head from this, you know. Not egotistically, but just, "Hey, I mean life can be beautiful, even though there are some incredible hardships and some incredible down times. There are ways of going through those." And the workshop was definitely a way of busting through.

After having left the workshop I was still very high. I was just high on that kind of positive energy level. Maybe those are just words, maybe I'm not being very clear. The thing I wanted to express is that this kind of feeling, this high, is a positiveness that lasted for a couple of weeks. And then when it did kind of burst, the bubble did burst open, and I sort of came down, I sort of gently eased myself down. That was because I realized I was in control, it was my choice. I was down, but I had a choice as to what I wanted to do with the experience I had just come from. And that's still with me, that kind of control, on a level that I hadn't experienced before. It's not on a verbal, a head kind of level, but on a gut level. I feel kind of solid in myself in that life and death are what they are, and that certain lessons come from certain kinds of situations. Certain beings bring to you whatever it is they bring to you, and how you deal with that is how you deal with that. I was finding out how I could deal with that, in a way that life could still have meaning and the warmth and the love that is always there. It just takes something to uncover it, expose it. It takes something on my part to want that.

And I feel that workshop and the other workshop with Kamala reinforced that, me wanting to be more responsible for my life in a way that I could feel good about living even though my son had died and my daughter is struggling with a life-and-death situation. And to sum all this up, I guess the biggest thing that happened from all this is a connection I've made with the spiritual quadrant in my beingness. My spirituality is something I have often thought about, but had never really approached or had the courage to investigate. And through you, through your workshop and through other things that have happened since the workshops, I find myself just sort of naturally seeking out religious, spiritual kinds of things; things that I'd always just avoided or condescended to. Well, not quite. I had never really given them that much validity. And now it's very different, very different and I feel it. I feel myself making that kind of connection with that kind of energy, with that kind of invisibleness, things I don't see, things that don't come in by the normal channels, the five senses. I'm allowing myself to approach that and to just make that connection.

I find myself doing that with Kamala more and more as I watch her going through her kinds of experiences, with her life. I see myself just loving her, just loving her, knowing that the best thing I can do for her is to love her unconditionally. Thank you, Elisabeth. I love you.

CHERYL

Hi, Elisabeth. You had wanted me to talk about my feelings before, during and after the workshop. The first time I met you, in the airport, I learned about divine manipulation.

When I first met you then, I was having a very difficult time being with Paul and the anger he had that was being directed out all over the place. There was no place really for me to go to feel comfortable, to have any space of my own to go through whatever I had to go through. I still don't understand a lot of that, but it all feels better now. I'm not sure how, or why. It's hard to relate to particular events.

When Paul and I went to that first workshop I found out about my doubts. I decided to leave my doubts there. I didn't need them. I was doubting in the universe, doubting in my capacity to live and love. God, a lot of stuff happened.

During that workshop I went through hell, and I don't have any other way to describe it. Really, it was seeing how I plague myself and I couldn't find any way to run away from it. And then at one point I realized that I have to just be in it and go through it, and I found that it passed. I found out about all the hurt, all the hurts of everybody on this planet. Going through their lives and the pain that they pick up, I saw how my life and the pain I was going through was a reflection of all that is in each one of us. And we can hurt ourselves, I can hurt myself as much as I want to; and I also had the capacity to not hurt myself if I choose not to.

The pain of my daughter first getting cancer,

and the shock of that, stayed with me for a very long time. I think somewhere in me I knew about this development, this new cancer at the time, and it was as if I was driven a lot of times to do just anything, to be active in some crazy way. It was a form of avoidance for me, avoiding the pain I was going through and the possible pain in the future. And then when Tyheen got sick and died, it was like my entire world fell apart. I didn't know where to go or who to turn to. I spent some time looking in on myself, and not understanding me or anything outside or around me.

When I went to the first workshop and saw these other people and loved these other people, and saw the loving and what that did to all of us, en masse, I realized that there is a transformation that comes from that love. I realized that we each have to pass through all the stages, all the emotions, turmoil and fear and sadness, in order to get to the other side and feel that love and see what that generates. And what that generates is peace, the only true feeling of well-being, and it doesn't come from outside events. I've learned peace the hard way.

Y. L. (another workshop participant) was an incredible experience for me. Through experiencing her, who she is, in some way I came to see myself as a baby just learning to crawl, the excitement of that, the ability to crawl and then for a moment, for a very wobbly moment, standing up and having that moment of incredible freedom, true inner freedom—standing up.

I went away from that workshop having relearned how to love, particularly loving myself and Paul, that wonderful person I share my life with. I felt that bonding of love between us, and that helped carry me through.

The second workshop, that Kamala went to and we were luxuriously able to join in on, came at a time when again I felt totally beaten down. I was filled with anger—anger at the universe for her pain and her suffering, and for my pain and suffering in having to view her pain twenty-four hours a day, to feel that. And I had a realization of Paul's original anger which he had before the first workshop. What I had done was turn my anger toward Kamala for her pain, knowing I was loving her and hating her at the same time. And I had a hard time living with myself, hating this incredible, beautiful person, my daughter. It was just very hard for me to accept that in myself.

And from that workshop, watching her amidst all these other people, seeing her for the first time in a long time blossoming and opening up to that love that was being generated towards her and through her for the first time in many months, again I felt a freedom within myself. I also, feeling her open to that, felt myself open to her.

It's still difficult now. It's not easy. She's sick and in pain a lot, and not able to move. But there's something that shines still, through her, and I can allow myself to see that. I can be thankful for all that we've had in the past and all that we have now, and for the beauty that this universe holds. I know that somewhere in me I feel comfortable. There is nothing that I can connect it with because I cannot relate that inner peace to my head. But I know that everything is okay and that it's leading somewhere that's correct.

And I want to thank you and everybody who

is with you, who are allowing these spaces to emerge, and all the people who come in contact with you, for the peace you've given to me and Paul and Kamala. The love just doesn't stop.

Kamala died a few weeks after she attended a workshop on her own. She made a lasting impression on all those who shared this last week away from home with her.

At first reticent, she finally was able to share her feelings with the group and opened not only her own heart, but the ones of all the participants.

By what some people may consider coincidence—we call it "divine manipulation"—I was fogged in in Oregon but was able to get a plane to San Francisco, where I called Cheryl and Paul, who picked me up at the airport where we first met some months ago. Kamala died that very afternoon and I had the privilege of staying at their home during the first night that Paul and Cheryl were childless.

We had a moving memorial at their home, after her body was removed and many wonderful friends from near and far joined us in this gathering. I spent the night in Kamala's bed and found the blue stuffed elephant under her bedsheets playing "you are my sunshine," a profound experience for me! We had given this elephant to her as a good-bye gift at the end of the workshop so that she could always hear one of our favorite songs. She had obviously held it in her arms when she made the transition.

Both Cheryl and Paul have kept in touch with us and they are touching many lives at present and help others who go through similar experiences. We are grateful to them for their courage to share in the midst of the windstorms of their young lives. No one has perhaps more verified my favorite saying: "Should you shield the canyons from the windstorms you would never see the beauty of their carvings."

13
Quadriplegics

※ ※

EILEEN

T IS VERY DIFFICULT to share some of the highlights of these workshop experiences in words, as all these things are experiences felt and shared on an experiential, almost nonverbal level. It is the intensity of love and care, courage and honesty, that is impressive, and anyone who has actively participated in these workshops will never be the same. The beauty of it is that it lasts only from Monday noon until Friday noon and yet it becomes a catalyst for a process that continues over months and years. Many people who attended one of these weeks years ago have continued to write us years later, sharing with us the enormous growth that was started at the workshop and that continues thereafter without counseling sessions or expensive therapy.

We have especially encouraged quadriplegics and paraplegics to attend our workshops. In my work with multiply handicapped children it had become evident that those who cannot use their limbs, those who are blind, those who are unable to hear and especially the ones who are quadriplegic are often treated as dependent, vulnerable beings who either have to be overprotected or shielded from any emotional reaction or have been so badly neglected that they became numb. They sometimes build up a tremendous shield around their feelings in order to appear stoical and insensitive, and at times seem arrogant and untouchable.

Our workshops have been a wonderful place for these frequently very young people to simply observe for the first two or three days the seventy or eighty participants who are not handicapped, and yet full of anguish, agony and pain with losses of a different nature but nevertheless as painful as theirs. When we sense their readiness to share their own anguish, we become their limbs, their hands, their legs, for them. For those who can't see, we become their eyes. And with the help of specially trained assistants we are able to compensate for whatever faculty they are unable to use themselves.

Here are a few commentaries of those who came to us. The first is from a quadriplegic in a wheelchair, who had great difficulties during the first workshop. Her letter reads

> This workshop has been very fruitful for me. My initial feeling on Friday was a quiet, deep peace, which is always a positive sign of something lasting for me. The peace has indeed endured, allowing me a more spontaneous flowing with all . . . also in touch with more personal power. I feel more centered.
>
> Elisabeth, I know you know I'm grateful for so much of what you have given. I guess I have a need to tell you that your very being blesses my life like no other.
>
> Once in a while in the quiet I think of you and how real, unpretentious and sometimes shy you are. At those times I sense a small connection with bits of the pain that comes with what you are called to do.
>
> The closeness I experienced with you this work-

shop was a bonus blessing. It tickled me to see you receiving more easily from people. My friend was even pleased to be able to get some coffee for you. The irony in all this is that there is even a giving in the receiving. And the circle flows on.

When I ponder the reasons for my life, I ask why I chose paralysis. The answer that keeps resounding is "to learn how to receive graciously." Seems simple? Well, I think you know how difficult that road has been, huh?

Good news! I remember sitting in your living room in Flossmoor, explaining to you why I couldn't take a plane to the West Coast. You leaned forward with a penetrating, affirming question, "You mean you'd let a little pain in your back control your future?" Well, I went, I grew, I got unstuck. Never realized how dependent I had become on my secure environment and community. Never would I have believed that almost a year after your challenging question I would be considering the possibility of staying on the West Coast for this coming winter. The odds seem horrendous, but inside I know now that I can do it. If it is in His plan, it will unfold.

Love, *Eileen*

I can't describe in words the changes that have taken place in Eileen and other people like Eileen who because of accidents or multiple sclerosis have been paralyzed and unable to move, who have depended on staff around the clock and who have adjusted to a life-style totally different from that of most of us. Many of our quadriplegics are terribly arrogant when they apply for the workshop. They demand special attention, or want to bring two or three personal attendants or nurses with them. They want their own private living or sleeping quarters. And they expect a special kind of treatment. When arrogance becomes an issue prior to their arrival, we have developed a very firm response to these people. We allow only one friend or nurse to come along. The rest of the care has to be accepted from the members of the workshop group, many of whom are physicians, psychiatrists, therapists, nurses, inhalation and rehabilitation therapists, all of whom are very qualified to take care of quadriplegic patients.

If the registrants are humble enough to accept these limitations, their prognosis is usually excellent, albeit their anger at me during the first day or two is extreme. Many of them do not even honor me by a look or by a spoken word. It is only after they get in touch with their own negativity that they are able to open up and then they gain a great deal from participation.

Here again our results have so very often been extremely positive that I know we are doing the right thing. I said earlier that I can't describe in words the changes that have taken place, for instance, in Eileen. I meant that. I can't. But Eileen can, in her own words. This remarkable letter, an incredible example of loving and caring, of understanding and growth, was received by me at Shanti Nilaya six months after Eileen attended her last workshop, in Madison, Wisconsin, in June 1980. It was to be read after her death, which came in November of 1980:

> To my family and dear friends,
>
> I want to say something simple, but you know me. . . . I asked that Maribeth read this . . . I can see you crying behind your smile, Mar . . . I love you!
>
> As I write this, I feel very small. . . . Aware of the me under this comfortable skin. Kathy Sullivan once said, "You know how comfortable

you are with the you under your skin . . . well, think of you that's more than you and that's God!" I sense a touch of that me today and feel humbled by the reality that without each of you I would never have known me . . . God in me!

Today I am more whole than I ever was in my body, more complete in Christ than I ever could have imagined. Each of you is a special significant part of me. In some way you have created me.

How can I thank you?

I am so free right now . . . I've danced (I'm a terrific dancer) . . . I've run in the rain, walked naked by the sea, warmed by God's great light: a light indescribable. I'm with you now, I taste your tears and feel your loss. I have a gift for you! The love I know at this moment is so pure, so completely void of negativity as to be instantly healing, affirming one to immediate greatness.

What a world this world would be if only every man and woman would let this love in, allow this love to control . . .

The gift! At this liturgy today as you celebrate my new life, I'm going to touch each of you with this love. God touching you through me. Don't worry. I've already asked. He said ok!

So, please, let go of any negativity, open your hearts, minds, souls, and feel loved by a great, gentle, gracious Father.

Yes, you can do it! Allow me to share this last touching with you, huh?

It's yours . . . believe it!

Eileen Marie Kral
May 7, 1940–November 15, 1980

GERI

Another quadriplegic friend of ours was Geri, who was born in Illinois as the younger of two siblings. The family moved around quite a bit while she was in elementary school, and then settled in the San Francisco area when she was about ten. She went to Occidental College when she was seventeen, the same year she was diagnosed as having multiple sclerosis, and never lived with her family after that on a permanent basis. She continued her education and got her master's degree and became a marriage, family and child counselor.

For fifteen years it was a slow but constant deterioration from walking to crutches, to wheelchair, to electric wheelchair, to not being able to move at all. When she attended our workshop the first time, she had been in an extremely depressed state, unable to show any emotions, and having lost a great deal of weight. She began also to lose her sight and by the time she attended her second workshop she was unable to see well enough to recognize people.

I asked Geri to share her own impressions of the two workshops she has attended, as she can better express what it is like from the participant's point of view.

> Hello, Elisabeth, haven't talked to you in a while. Let me start out by explaining what was going on with me before the first workshop, which was October 1977. I was in a place where I didn't really want to live any more. Doctors had told me enough discouraging news that I didn't really want to have to deal with breathing machines or tracheotomy or anything like that. So I had started to take matters into my own hands. I even stopped eating and had lost—I don't know—probably forty to fifty pounds. I started doing that in Jan-

uary of 1976. That was a slow, gradual process and was very hard to do because everybody had to feed me and I had to manipulate it so nobody knew I wasn't eating.

Prior to the workshop in October I had begun to eat again. But not with much gusto. I was still getting reports from doctors that my breathing was in terrible shape and that I was going to have to be on machines. Nobody told me that I was going to die, but it all spelled death to me. And so after hearing you at the AHP convention in Los Angeles I wanted to go to your workshop, because I thought, granted, I was going to die, but what should I do between now and death? I didn't know how to live my life.

Interestingly enough, I was really, really terrified about going to the workshop. And when people asked me what I was afraid of, I would say, "I'm going to die. I'm going to go there and I'm going to die." I didn't know what was going to happen to me, just that something would change.

And something really did change, because I discovered at the workshop that I was indeed alive and that there were things to live for. I'm not sure what made me realize that. I think it had something to do with people responding to me, not just because I had MS [Multiple Sclerosis]. It seemed that suddenly there were a lot of people who meant a lot to me. And the sharing of others' pain made me feel like I was not alone. My struggle was not totally solitary. And that was very freeing.

I remember that I had a hard time crying. I felt like a fraud because I thought that I didn't feel things that I ought to. I remember your saying to me that probably I had learned very early to conceal my feelings and that for me to start feeling would be a slow process and probably a painful one. So I went away from that workshop higher than a kite, actually, because I had suddenly discovered that there was a life to live.

When I got home there was one interesting reaction to the workshop. For the next several months I got everything in order, to enable me to die properly. I got a conservator, I made sure that my doctor and hospital knew that I would not subject myself to machines. And I was really into it. I'm not sure I actually considered whether or not I was going to die, or whether it was imminent, but it was something that I had to finish. Having started to *live* at the workshop, I had to complete the death of the old way of being. If that's clear at all, I don't know. I had to kill off the old Geri, and I think I did that in spades.

I attended another of your lectures in either February or March of 1979. And after that you invited me to the workshop in May. My reaction to your invitation was kind of interesting, because I immediately thought, "No, I can't go, I'm too busy. I've work to do, I can't take the time off." And then I had to stop and think, "What was I afraid of, why did I really not want to go to the workshop?"

I discovered that I still felt very much like a fraud and I knew that it was time to give that up. But that would be very difficult for me to give up. After all, being "star cripple" had been my way of being for years. I got a lot of attention that way, but it wasn't working for me.

Being "star cripple" kept me very far from my

feelings and was a very demanding role for me to have. It was exhausting to do as many activities as I was, and I knew that I would have to stop being so busy. Stopping that meant that I had to find another way of being, because I knew that when I was not busy I would get depressed. I couldn't stand to be with myself doing nothing because it meant that *I* was nothing. So I knew I had work to do. I didn't know how I was going to go about it, of course.

The workshop was a surprise. I sat there for a couple of days rather calm through the sharing of other people's pain. But it was getting to me, I guess. And then suddenly I started being out of control, but only in the situation of my friend, Jaima, taking me to the ladies' room. She would take me to go pee, and I would burst into tears. I had no idea what was going on with me. I didn't know what I was crying about.

Then one evening, I think it might have been Wednesday, the group had broken for dinner and I had to go pee. And of course, I ended up crying. Jaima asked me whether I wanted to go to dinner or do some work and I kind of mumbled, "No, I think I'm all right, I'll go to dinner." And then, leaving the ladies' room, we went into the courtyard and the chimes were going, and the chimes made me cry. Everything seemed to make me cry. So Jaima took me back into one of the small rooms, and they went to get you.

I was absolutely unable to stop crying, and just one thought would lead to another, which led to another, and to each one I responded with tears. Then Jaima had gotten me out of my chair and onto a mat. And when you came in you got down

on the mat with me and I just started to talk. I
was surprised at some of the things I said. I spoke
about my mother and the guilt I've felt about her
death. And that I have never known how to touch
people, and now when I wanted to I couldn't.

And all of a sudden there was all the sadness
that I had kept hidden behind the disguise of "star
cripple." I knew I had made changes in the first
workshop and I could have rested on my laurels.
But that's not why I had come.

There was something about the discovery of
sadness that opened up a whole world to me. After
I got home I continued to cry when people took
me to pee. And it expanded to when people brushed
my teeth or combed my hair, and it was very
obviously the personal things that made me cry
and made me get in touch with the fact that I
could not do these things for myself.

I've had multiple sclerosis for fifteen years and
I never, never let myself feel that sadness. In fact,
for the first three or four years I had such a thing
about self-pity that I would berate myself if I got
upset about anything. And that became a pattern
that just totally ran me for a long time. And the
discovery of sadness, more so than the discovery
of joy, made me more alive.

The first workshop gave me happiness, it made
me want to live. The second workshop gave me
some dimension, some understanding of the real
struggle that I had. I can't kick myself anymore,
I can't pretend that I don't have MS or that I'm
just like everybody else. It is a struggle and it is
sad, there is a lot of loss. I no longer play with
the idea of death being right around the corner
bailing me out of this mess. I'll have to live with

it. And it is very hard for me at times, but I think I am more real with it.

At the first workshop was someone who had lost a child, fairly young. The mother was talking and beating the mattress about it. For whatever reason, it stirred up in me a *lot* of feeling and I started crying hysterically. It had something to do with the mother using terms that I had just recently learned, like postural drainage, things like that. I knew that I wished my parents had cared as much as those two people had cared about Laura. That day, that morning, kind of broke the ice for me. I couldn't stay so bottled up as I had been.

In a similar way, in the second workshop there was a woman who had a husband who was in a nursing home with MS. I felt myself gasp when she said that, because that is the fear that I live with all the time, that I will at some point end up in a nursing home. Because of that I made a *direct* tie with this woman.

I'm not sure why I started getting so upset about peeing. All I know is that there was an awful lot of really intense sharing of pain the day that I started getting upset. And I guess I couldn't tolerate my own pain. My defenses were down.

There is something about people talking very personally about their own tragedy or their own vulnerability that will set off a kind of chain-reaction effect. You know, large groups, not just the one in the workshop. And so, suddenly it feels as though you're in a room of pain. The pain itself is not frightening. I mean, everybody is sharing together. And so it is not something that we turn away from. There is a sort of invitation and permission to let yourself say the unsayable, feel what you don't want to feel, because others are.

There is something about even the introductions, saying who you are and something about yourself and strengths and weaknesses, that programs from the outset that you be honest with the group. There is no facade, no artificiality or anything like that. There is no social role stuff going on, you are just who you are. And there is something about *that much honesty*—you can't escape it. You're right there with yourself and you can't avoid it.

There was something in the first workshop that continues to amaze me. It seemed in the first day and a half or so that the group was not becoming cohesive. And there was a sense of frustration in the group. I know I was feeling it, and some other people were talking about it. One participant started to talk about it, and about the difficulty she was having with the smokers in the room, or something like that. She got into some material of her own saying something about not having a choice. I do not usually become an active member in a group; I'm an observer, I sit back and I just watch. And there this participant was talking and the rest of the group was very quiet, because what do you do with the problem with smokers and nonsmokers? And I suddenly found this voice of mine saying that you always have a choice.

And there was something in my having said that, that suddenly made the whole group interact. I don't claim to understand what happened, but it seemed to change the nature of that group. I don't know what made me say that, as I don't usually talk in groups. But I did.

People are not used to being open with feelings that are less than wonderful—hurt, fear, sadness or resentment, guilt, anger, all those things. People like to keep in the closet. But they were out there because the invitation was there. I can almost picture in my head that you are only half a person without those emotions. And when you include them you become whole. It is the sense of that wholeness, that completeness, that's kind of like in music when suddenly there is a major chord after a whole bunch of minors. It is just very satisfying, it's complete, it's whole. And I think that is what makes it such an amazing experience.

The difference between the first workshop and the second was that in the second the screaming was invited, and I think it is a very useful tool. Everybody has a scream, somewhere for some reason, and some part of them that wants to yell out for something. And that scream is in a way such a primeval thing that the scream itself frees people, opens up the door to all those hidden, ucky feelings. There was always something really appealing to me about that painting called *The Scream*. The artist depicted artistically a scream. It is very hard to picture in your head what a scream would look like, but he did it. And the scream was almost tangible at the workshop. There was something that was very positive because it was the link between you and the more real you. And it was very freeing.

It is interesting to me that I look at what happened as being a kind of group contagion thing. But that doesn't explain an individual's choice to be first. All I can say is, either whoever went first was very brave and very much in touch with whatever was going on with them, or there was something else going on. But as I said, the invitation was there. So it was more than group contagion, it was your expectations.

You said we have four days, and so everybody was given a kind of assignment. You have four days to, in essence, "clean up your act." So not only was it an invitation, it was in a way a challenge and it was expected.

It was a very protected environment, everyone was kind of watched out for. Somebody on the staff was ready to work with anybody in the group. They were all very watchful of what was going on with people who were not at the time on the mattress but might be having some reaction. Then much care was taken that nobody be hurt physically. When people start to flail and beat things, it is very easy for somebody to back up into a chair, hit their head on something. Very much care was taken to make sure that didn't happen. It was very impressive. And it was another way that you knew you were safe, that you can do anything and it would be safe.

Now, after the second workshop, I hold the experience as being much more personal than I did after the first one. After the first I wanted to talk to everybody and spread the word, and just yak to death. If I look at it kind of clinically, it was as if I wanted to get rid of the experience. The second workshop I want to hold on to. I don't want to talk freely about it, or I feel as though what happened is so personal that it's hard to just tell. It's hard to just say, "Oh, hey, I had five days in Oceanside, let me tell you what happened to me!"

Because what happened is on many different levels, I still have not totally incorporated the things that I realized there. And for a while I was very kind to myself and was doing less. Now I'm finding myself wanting to be busy again. I'm very suspicious of that, but at least I know what I'm doing.

I can't say that the workshop made me happy with my situation. It made me unafraid. If anything it kind of intensified all the feelings that I had concealed. But if I hadn't felt them and explored them, I feel that I would have exploded at some point.

One thing that remains for me out of my experience, that we haven't talked about, is the power of the shift in the middle of the workshop, or after two-thirds of the workshop—the shift from the focus on the negative feelings, the pain and the need to let go of that and move into the joy, and moving into the positiveness and the forward-looking and life-giving qualities of life. You played on that in those first days, that you've only got so much time to get rid of this pain, deal with the pain. In the first workshop, I really felt the shift. I really felt kind of a shedding of negativity midway through the week, and very much lighter and freer toward the end. The second picture that I drew at that first workshop was of balloons. And that's what I felt, light and just floating.

In the second workshop, I didn't have that. There was a lightness that I felt, just because I opened myself up. There was a freeing of all that energy tied up in staying shut down. But all that stuff that I let out was scary stuff for me. I couldn't be really light with it. It was as though I had started a process of getting reacquainted with me, and it was what you had talked about the first time, that when I got in touch with my feelings it would be a long process, probably painful. And that is what happened. So I didn't experience the lightness, but I guess I experienced a *realness* of me. It was the first time in a long time that I didn't feel like a fraud. I was honest with myself.

I think maybe I should include that I am still a skeptic. I don't believe in, I don't know, curative powers. I kind of believe in the gods, but not all the time, and I don't believe that I will get better. Somehow the workshop helped me realize that it was irrelevant whether I got better or not. What was relevant was that I have MS, now how am I going to live with it. And I know the holistic health bit about mind and body and spirit, all that stuff that if I could just get it in order, I wouldn't have MS. I don't really believe that.

Having made that choice to be skeptical, or to doubt or whatever, all I have is my day-to-day reality, and that's enough for me. I don't want to spend time wondering about whether I'm going to get better or not. It takes up too much time, I have other things to do. So, some people criticize me because I don't do physical therapy and I'm not up on the latest diets or vitamins or what-have-you. But I would rather spend time doing what I want to do, what I enjoy doing, and not be so concerned with the MS. There's more to life besides MS.

Just prior to the first workshop I started working with groups of people with MS at UCLA. I continue doing that, and I feel much different now in those groups. I don't feel like Therapist (capital *T*). I'm a participant, I share with them now. I may be the leader of the group, but I've got MS too, and I have my own experience. Before when I was being a Therapist I would not use myself; I would be a kind of textbook therapist. And now I can share myself. I think that the workshops helped me do that, because they stripped a lot of that fraud from me.

OTTY

Another of our most moving experiences was given to us as a gift by a beautiful person named Otty. This account was handwritten on yellow lined paper and given to me. Of course, I remember the incident very well, and I saved that yellow lined paper for a very long time so that I could share Otty's story as part of this book:

During the workshop, listening to others work, very strong feelings of anger, abandonment, rejection, and self-hate started stirring in me. Many of these feelings had to do with the fact that I had an ileostomy at the age of 16 years. I spoke with you at lunch, and you said what I needed to do was to show everyone the ileostomy! (There were about 75 people in the group.) I panicked and said no. The thought of "exposing" myself was so terrifying that I did not attend the next scheduled session.

The next morning I went to the session, and when it was time to start working, you signaled for me to come up to where you were. I very reluctantly went, vowing to myself that I would not do what you had suggested. You asked me to tell everyone what it felt like to have the ileostomy. Hanging on to your hand, I related to the group my feelings of shame and disgust, the feeling of being less than human. What I said triggered something in one of the other participants. He was a young man who was in a wheelchair. I believe he had MS. He was unable to function from the waist down and was extremely weak and thin. He pulled his wheelchair up to the mat and with every ounce of strength he had, fell on the mattress in front of the group and desperately tried to pound the rubber hose as he cried and shouted out his feelings of anger, helplessness and all the frustration he was feeling.

After he had exhausted himself, he got back into his wheelchair and, suddenly, after having shared what he went through, it became okay for me to share and show my ileostomy. Since we were in the middle of a field, under a tent, arrangements were made to take me back to the house as soon as I was through, so I could replace the appliance I would have to take off in order to show the stoma.

As I took off the appliance, you told the group that those who couldn't look could leave and those who threw up you would work with later.

You had everyone come up close, and as they looked at me, more exposed than I have ever felt in my life, you had me look into everyone's eyes. What I saw was love and acceptance.

When I got back to the house, I went into the bathroom to put on a new appliance. There was a mirror in the bathroom, and for the first time in over 30 years, I was able to look at my body in the mirror without the appliance, and know that it was not the ugly sight I had believed it to be.

On returning to the group, many came over to me to say how much I had helped them by what I had done.

14

Suicide, Self-Acceptance and Letting Go

🌿

About suicide and suicide prevention
self-worth and letting go of pain . . .

TANYA

NOT ALL PARTICIPANTS have had such profound positive experiences at our workshops. The hardest hit and least resolved are often those whose children have committed suicide.

It is hard to accept that our own expectations and our own need to have our children gratify our own needs makes the loss of such a child even more unbearable.

All those who came to look at their own unfinished business left with more awareness, beginning to understand that we have to live our own lives, that we have free choice to lay claim to our own emotions and that we can face life as a challenge and not as a threat.

In our last Ramona workshop we had seven suicidal patients, and six left nonsuicidal.

This is a letter from a distraught mother whose son, a psychiatrist, committed suicide.

> I don't know how to express my appreciation and my thanks to you. I don't want to talk too much so I'll try to get right to it.
>
> You asked me what I expected when I first heard about Shanti Nilaya, and what I antici-

pated. I found out about Shanti Nilaya from
C. G. We were in a woman's support group together. Her daughter had died, and she and her
husband were in your workshop some time ago.
They gave me your private number and when I
reached you and told you what had happened with
my son you said, "You come here. We will help
you." I'm not saying it quite like you did, but
just the sound of your voice, talking to you, gave
me some sense of hope. You seemed so sure that
something was going to change the way I was
feeling.

On the day of your workshop I drove down,
driving thirty-five miles an hour, crying and hating everybody I saw. All the men, I could have
killed them if I had a chance, and I couldn't
imagine that my son wasn't seeing all the things
I was seeing. He used to love the drive, and he
loved San Diego. We'd made this drive so many
times when he was a child, and as he was growing
up he drove himself.

I had lost all fear with his death. But nothing
mattered. I was just numb and very angry, not
really feeling alive. When I drove up to the mission, all the angers I had been accustomed to
feeling, of the Spaniards coming in and taking
the land from the Indians, were of no conse-
quence. There was a building, there was land. It
was California, there were people, there was some
sort of purpose in the place where our retreat was
going to be held. That was all I could imagine.

And Mal was there, and he was unloading your
car. I didn't know who he was at the time, but
I saw this gentle face and he smiled to me. I
thought, "What's that man smiling at me for?

Why is he looking at me nicely?" And then I got my luggage and went in, and there was Boots. As always, she was loving and comforting and reached out to me. She said where my room would be and I felt much better after seeing her, and I went inside.

I don't remember anything more except I knew that there was some purpose in all those people being together. And I knew that your voice, your strength and your integrity would tie us together and help us.

I would like to talk about what I experienced in the workshop. Your first introductory lecture brought your whole self to us, to me, and relaxed any apprehension I might have had as you shared how you had lost your identity as a triplet. Somehow it made it possible for you to blend with all of us, to shift roles, take different places, push us here and push us there to guide us, lead us without any pain. I received love and caring from you in what you shared with us. You made us a family and told us that we were brought together for a purpose, that we had things to do.

I think that the unity we shared as a group, even with our differences, made us really cohesive. We could work together in trust because we knew that whatever we did could help another person, I could empathize with other people's feelings and could see where they had been, what had happened to them. All through everything I kept thinking of my son. Wondering why he couldn't have been there, how it would have helped him, why aren't doctors helped, how can doctors be helped, why aren't they given alternatives.

All risk, all fear of risk was dissolved. I felt

totally supported by the love from you, and I felt secure in every way in the surroundings. All my attention was somehow focused only on being where I was at the time. I didn't have to make excuses for anything. I didn't have to worry about anything. The children were safe and I could just really feel whatever I felt at the moment.

I haven't come to terms with my son's death. I believe too many things could have helped him to go on living. I remember you saying, "Take the shit and use it for fertilizer. Be a good gardener." This is very important. I realized when I was there at Shanti Nilaya that I wanted to be part of Shanti Nilaya. I took home your courage, your use of fertilizer, your personal determination to outlast and overcome all obstacles.

You said that reentry is the most difficult, and it was true. Reentry into the so-called real world is difficult, where everyone is so unreal and so afraid of their feelings. I don't know what my purpose is, I don't know where I'm going to go or what I'm going to do. It is my hope that someday maybe I could do something for Shanti Nilaya.

I can't say enough for Mal. He smiled at me when I first came in. And all the way through the workshop he gently encouraged me. He treated me with such kindness and respect and interest, and seemed to value what I had to say and who I was, that it gave me a feeling of reassurance that I had some value.

I'm grateful to everyone, especially, for the encouragement to cry, to scream, not to hold things back. I didn't want to disturb anyone when we were all together. I was told, "No, let it out. You're not disturbing anybody." And now I can open my mouth and cry, and I can say what I feel.

What was really important of my experience in the workshop is that I could truly express my grief, the grief that my loss was my total life. All that I could feel of my life was the loss of my son. I could really not have any distraction from that. But in the workshop all the things that were required of me as a separate person were set in abeyance and I was allowed to feel the pain. Nothing could have actually stopped the feeling of the pain; but by being able to express it, I had some feelings of life. Also, through expressing my grief and my feelings, I felt my son's life.

When I came back home and, as you say, made a reentry, there was no feeling of contact with Creed. No one talked about him. There was no one who wanted to say anything to me. I withdrew into my own life with my children and all my girls couldn't talk to me. No one seemed to recognize what was happening. It was as though everyone was walking around with their eyes closed, looking at other things, and only I was feeling Creed's loss.

The girls would scream at me when I cried. One girl would scream at me to stop it and not to do that. She couldn't stand it. My eldest daughter totally refused to say anything. Once or twice she talked, and she said that Creed's behavior was crazy and she didn't want any part of that craziness and wasn't going to talk to me if I behaved that way. She not only turned me off, she behaved as though Creed didn't exist.

Only my youngest daughter allowed me to cry. But if I was crying while driving she would say,

"Mother, you're driving in the car. Stop crying. You're in the present now. Creed is dead. Don't do that, Mother." It was as if she was mothering me for a long time, and I had no control. Everyone wanted to say, "Now, you just get over it. Everything's all right. Just forget it now, and get busy." I couldn't get busy for a long time.

During the workshop I was allowed to grieve very actively and in whatever manner I wanted to express myself. When I went home to my family and friends, where I wasn't allowed to continue this grieving, it was inhibiting. I felt stymied and it was very difficult for me to cope with the everyday life. The five days I was in the workshop, where I was allowed to grieve and where I was with people who understood, it was like whetting my appetite. It was helping me, but the five days weren't really enough. I wanted this grieving to go on; I needed this for a longer period, to be surrounded and to feel the support.

I felt that I wanted to go back to the workshop, it was the only safe place for me. Nothing was safe away from Shanti Nilaya. People not only didn't understand, but they weren't real themselves. I felt that people didn't realize how important being honest with others was, not only in regard to me but in their own manner of living. I couldn't see the value of talking to people because it didn't feel real. It was difficult to perform just going through the actions of something. It was just too hard for me to move for a long time. I really wanted to come back.

I had thought this workshop was a way I could get some help and I didn't realize how high my expectations were. I remember that when I first heard about Elisabeth, I immediately thought, "Oh, there's some ray of hope that I can survive Creed's death!" So many people were coming over and telling me what to do and nothing was right. I had heard about Elisabeth Kübler-Ross, about death and dying, somewhere; it never really interested me deeply, wasn't a part of my life. But I thought perhaps she would be someone I could trust because she had so much experience. The ministers I had talked to just failed me terribly.

I truly felt that she had some sort of a mystique, some magic that she would have into my son's life, to tell me something I didn't know. I thought that then I could go ahead and make a life, because I couldn't in any way envision any kind of life for me. It was as though I had been dismembered and I could see no way of putting myself together, of pulling my life together. After seeing you, I really believed it was possible for you to do some of those things. I had some questions, I had some doubt because I saw you as a human being and I realize all human beings are fallible.

I think I imbued you with superhuman powers and thought anything you would do would be all right. You would make everything all right, you would have all the answers to all the questions.

I didn't get an answer to what had happened to Creed. I didn't get an answer as to where he was, you know, for my own understanding. I didn't find a way I could reach him. I knew that I went home unfulfilled and that I felt it would be a long search for me, a continuing search. I had hoped that I would be able to reach him. Yes. In some way.

One of the things in the workshop that was

really helpful to me was one time when I was walking and I felt like Creed was walking. I remembered Creed's walking, and it was like I was walking like Creed. When I was sitting in the circle I always sat in the front row. I imagined him being in the seminar, in the workshop. I felt close to him at that time because of the thinking of the people, knowing there were doctors present. But I kept not understanding why he couldn't have participated, why he couldn't have had this experience. Because this experience could have saved his life. I couldn't understand why this isn't presented for more people. It was really important to me. I could feel him. I don't know if I sensed him participating with me, but I imagined how he would have been within the situation. I think that was it. I imagined myself as myself in the same kind of a situation.

I would have liked to go to things like that with him, because they were opportunities for growth. I was angry with myself for not saying, "Why don't you take me along . . . ?" Because all the mail would come and I would see the advertisements for the seminars and never even thought of participating in them. I never realized that this type of thing was available to other people. I thought only doctors had this opportunity. I felt deprived. I feel deprived.

I hadn't thought about my own death. Then I realized, and I realize more and more, that Creed's death is also my death and that a lot of my life is gone with him. I feel less than half alive.

Before the workshop I tried to keep everything pleasant and conceal things from my children. By doing that I don't think I gave an authentic example, I didn't give them alternatives. I was a plastic person. I was always nice. I always had a lot of tears inside that I didn't share, a lot of anger. I didn't know I was angry. I felt he had cheated me and I feel responsible.

When my children asked me what's the matter I didn't say what was wrong. I'd say, "Oh, nothing. Everything's all right."

I invested so much of my life in Creed. And my expectations of him were so great! My life was totally involved in what he had accomplished. I think this is the thing that has been so hard for me. I have to refocus and find out some way to live my own life. I never had to before because Creed was all my expression. I functioned as a mother, taking care of things; but all inside I knew that Creed was living his own life and I could do the things I had to because he was really accomplishing. He was a free, successful, serving person. This was really important for me. I think if I could find some way that my life would have meaning, in the way I felt Creed's life had meaning, that would make me comfortable.

Creed's death doesn't destroy what he did. And when you talked to me yesterday you said that he's working very hard to help me, and my guides will help me to be better. I want it confirmed in some way so that I can know it. You said you wanted me to come down to Shanti Nilaya to the workshop. I told you my twelve-year-old daughter has to be driven back and forth to school and you said, "Your guides will help you, everything will fall into place so you can come down." And just by you saying that, immediately I felt that it was real. Whatever you say, I believe.

At the workshop one of the young women there said that she understood what I was saying when I started speaking in Russian. You had observed that she was very upset at this particular time. So you had her get on the mat and tell you what happened. She started to tell you and then she stopped. You said to me to sing in Russian. I started singing Russian songs and the girl started to release a lot of things and she went through a lot of emotion, a great deal. And you kept encouraging me. At that time I felt very useful. It was such a natural thing for me to do. It was nothing, it is just an adjunct to my own personality, a part of me. And in being of service like that I felt really important. A vital part of me was like a stream of light going from me.

Prior to this I had taught the group to sing a song in Russian. As I taught them the words and was leading them, the energy and the song and the music was a very powerful feeling, and this gave me a lot. I refocused on me in a different way. It was as though there was energy for me to do something, some part of me that was useful. It was nothing really that I did, it just did it through me automatically. I liked that because I wasn't creating something, I wasn't trying to manipulate anything, it just happened! With the lack of manipulation, by flowing naturally I felt really good.

I think the most important thing that I felt most was when you said to take *s-h-i-t* and turn it into fertilizer, that we have to be good gardeners. At the time you said that, that was the height of my personal experience. And when you introduced this to the group you also related the one about where he said "come to the edge"* and everyone said "no," and the third time he pushed them and they flew. I think these two things meant more to me in my own experience because they awakened something in me that I could work with. They were different than what I had done for myself, and when I was singing, it was a pleasant experience. But this gave me a new kind of strength that I could use those words and maybe I would fly and not fall off the edge. I felt I could take the pain in my life and turn it into some kind of blessing. It gave me hope. Your stories and examples gave me hope that there was a place for me and that there was something I could do.

Those were the high points. It is like they were something that was already there, and the light was shone on it. It was much different. It was very, very positive. I didn't see where I was going, I didn't see the direction. But I knew that that was the truth. I *know*.

I don't walk quickly, I drive my feet. I have to be invited continually to come to the edge. I

---

* The exact wording of one of our favorite sayings is:

> The Appolonaire said: "Come to the edge!"
> "No, we cannot, we are afraid."
> "Come to the edge!"
> "No, we cannot, we'll fall."
> "Come to the edge!"
> And they came, and he pushed them and they flew!

It contains an important message besides the obvious one, namely, that we should never ask or challenge anyone more than three times. If we exceed that in any situation of life, we impose our own needs, thus depriving our fellowmen of the greatest gift God gave to us—free choice!

have flown a couple of times and each time I fly back; and each time I have to drag myself up again and be encouraged to move ahead. But each time I know it is possible. It doesn't stay long. If there is no reinforcement I fall flat on my face. But your call in itself was a tremendous step. You know, awakening again that thing flying.

I am reminded that I can fly, and I'm reminded of the courage I know I expressed with myself about being there. It really wasn't anything; I mean, I had to do it to save my life. I had to do it. But I know that I did accept the invitation to come to the place.

I know that when we were having the bonfire, a lot of people by that time were finally taking courage to speak. And you had to stop it. There were eighty people up there with pine cones and it could take hours. So you finally said, "You had your opportunity before! Make a choice." And I waited because I didn't know what to say. I really didn't know; there was nothing I wanted to leave behind. I really had left it behind at the workshop and I could see there were so many people finally revealing themselves, awakening. And I realized that what I wanted the pine cone to do was not burn the past, because I didn't want to destroy or forget my past, but to lighten my weight in my steps ahead. And I couldn't see more than one step. One little pine cone in the dark isn't going to do a great deal. But I realized at that moment that there was some kind of instinctive hope.

Before the workshop my anger was so extreme. I used to be such a very pleasant person, and I suddenly didn't give a damn about anybody. I didn't care who felt what, how they felt about anything. I just didn't really care! And it was so total. I was just so different; every feeling I had was different—my concern, my sensitivity. I was furious.

I didn't want to run everybody off the road on the way to Escondido, but if they dropped dead I would say *"Yahoo!"* But it wouldn't have brought Creed back to me so it didn't matter. I had no balance in my emotions. Nothing was rational. I saw these people that were gathering and I wondered why Creed wasn't there. Nothing made sense to me.

One of the things that really impressed me was that I realized how important it was to express anger, to be aware of our feelings when we have them. I have submerged so much it was just like I could barely get my nose up out of the water, as it were, without completely drowning. I guess I had been drowned in my own inability to express myself for so long. I felt that I had confused my children and the people that were in my life because I didn't express the things that were troubling me. I didn't even know I was troubled. So that was the one thing I thought about and I see more and more.

I see the effects of my being able to release my anger now. And I know now what I didn't know then about my feelings. I didn't know what feelings I had. So I think that what I saw you doing with the whole group, and what I feel must be done in medical schools, has to be done. I think it probably has to be done in many, many situations. Give people an opportunity to really touch into themselves. And I think the only way we're going to do anything to help out the whole world is for not only ourselves, but anybody, to just be able to release this kind of violence that we feel. Otherwise we turn it onto ourselves and it affects other people in our lives. I think pragmatically that's the thing that was most helpful to me.

And I think it is important that this be done in a safe environment. I think we need nurturing in order to do it. (I realize that the first workshop, the psychodrama, was part of that; but I didn't trust the people there in the same way that I trusted you.) With you, I gave my whole heart and soul without any hesitation.

I think the experience with Y. L. there was very powerful. Her suffering was not only about the grief of her husband and her child, but she was having epileptic fits, seizures, constantly. And there was remarkable work done with her. Those things were just incredible, to see how someone else struggles and survives, and struggles and survives, and struggles and survives. To see the elasticity of the human being was remarkable for me.

It was not just watching you work with others that gave me the confidence to believe and trust. No, it was your love, not only your ability. It was your *love* of each human being, and the knowing how to work with that person, knowing the right words to say. Knowing when to pull back, when to do exactly what you were doing. I could completely trust myself with you because I believed.

BARBARA

My mother and I sat together Thanksgiving Eve talking about how much we missed one another since I'd moved from my hometown several years ago.

She never wanted to talk about getting older.
She'd touch on it with a joke; but this night she
was ready to share those feelings and fears—I
wasn't.

I cherished this visit with my mother and the
special days we now had, to talk, laugh and discover a new friendship.

Our relationship was not always so close. We
had many years of growing pains, filled full of
disappointment, criticism and expectation. Both
of her parents had died suddenly and tragically
and her marriage to my father was difficult.

I was the child born to fulfill her dreams, and
therefore her expectations were high and disappointments great. All my life I fought to be independent of her, as much as I needed, wanted
and loved her caring and love for me.

In early June, I received a call saying that my
mother had a slight heart attack and that I should
wait before coming. A short time passed and another call to say that she'd had a massive attack,
that I should be told the truth, and to come quickly.
I'll always be grateful for the honesty of that second call.

I spent that week in disbelief that all of those
medical devices could be attached to her body and
believed only that she would get well, leave soon,
and that we'd be talking and laughing together
in no time.

I was told by relatives to smile, to say that my
unhappy marriage was great, better than ever,
and not to touch her.

But just as I never expected her to die, neither
did they, and so they went on with their work,
on with their criticism, on with talking only of

pleasant things—waiting for another day, when the time was right to touch, to cry and to talk about fear.

On that last evening, I kissed her good night, she looked at me a long time and said, "Goodbye, precious, thank you." Two hours later she died.

When I arrived at the hospital, the nurses with lowered eyes over an evening pizza, were silent. A large carton sat near her bed. I resented the swiftness with which they had removed and packed her things. I didn't realize until later that this is standard hospital procedure and a way of "giving support."

She was lying peacefully and it felt so comfortable to climb into bed, snuggle to her and talk.

As I looked at her again, I now noticed large bruises and bumps on her head and was told that I'd have to wait until morning to find out what had happened. It was finally explained that she was left alone on a commode, fell over and died. Even though she'd been out of intensive care for only several hours, being left alone like this was standard hospital procedure.

Later that day, I realized that I couldn't call my mother at work, that she wasn't at home, and I didn't know where she was. No one had mentioned that someone was supposed to contact a funeral home. I called the hospital to ask where my mother was. "Refrigeration" was the answer. And so began the fright, the isolation, the longing and the loneliness.

During those days of the funeral, gathering Mom's belongings and leaving the house that would never again be filled with family celebrations, doctor friends tucked unrequested prescriptions into my hand—pills to dull the senses, loss and grief.

I began to associate tenderness with pain and closeness with loss. I spent days, then weeks, looking for a miracle, the missing piece that would bring her back.

I became more and more withdrawn, disoriented and lonely. When I returned home, I wasn't able to work, to teach, to mother, to look into the eyes of friends or to understand how everything continued on when my mother had died. The more people expected of me, the more I lost sight in believing in my own purpose and daily living. Those prescriptions were becoming more important.

One morning a friend called and mentioned a doctor named Elisabeth, who gave workshops around the world for people like me. I called the office at Shanti Nilaya, was told that the workshop was filled with a waiting list and that they would contact me if there was an opening. A short time later "Boots" called back to say she'd "squeezed me in." After getting to know Boots, her intuitiveness was just one of the special qualities she shared.

I arrived at the workshop distant, withdrawn and very depressed. During those days I cried and cried all those tears that I held deeply inside—for my best friend who drowned, for a childhood filled with the pain of unhappy parents, a father whose anger and criticism colored my days, for a brother I'd never get to know and for my mother whom I'd known for such a brief time and loved very much.

Elisabeth, her staff and seventy-five others listened and gave to me time, patience, tenderness and all the freedom to express myself without guilt or shame, and the strength to leave behind those prescriptions.

That was the beginning of believing in myself and renewed belief in life and love.

Within these past two years, I have come to understand more about what happens to people and their lives when they are isolated in living or in dying.

Now, along with my creative work, the mothering of my children and the joy of a loving relationship, I am a counselor with a very special volunteer group that gives support to individuals and families who are grieving.

I wish to say thank you to my friends for listening, to these counselors who devote time, sensitivity and use their own life experiences as a tool to support others and one another and to Elisabeth for teaching all of us to live and love and die with honesty.

Love, *Barbara*

Barbara, who had never taken drugs or tranquilizers before in her life and was shocked about the easy availability of same, was happy to throw the bottles of tranquilizers into the fire during our Thursday night ritual. Another tragedy prevented and the beginning of a new life and a wonderful new friendship.

CAROLYN

One of my most memorable experiences was a multiple sclerosis patient who wrote me a very moving letter many

years ago after seeing me in one of my lectures on the West
Coast. She wanted to end her life and was very despondent.
I corresponded with her and encouraged her to share her
pain and her agony, not to despair and not to regard suicide
as a solution, as it is never a solution.

She wrote:

> After attending your workshop today on "Death
> and Dying," I have just returned to my office
> after leaving a moving and emotionally draining
> but tremendously rewarding day at the Institute.
> I guess you might say I have come to my own
> screaming or crying room.
>
> Each day for the past few weeks I have been
> more and more fully aware of death and dying,
> living by somehow existing or "resignation," as
> you called it. Today was the culmination of many
> feelings, reactions and trips I have been through,
> and it felt as though you were taking me by the
> hand through all of them all over again.
>
> As I have worked in rehabilitation counseling,
> I have gradually become aware of my complete
> lack of exposure, understanding and experience
> in dealing with death and dying. Always I have
> pushed it off to some distant time when I would
> come to grips with it. But not now!
>
> Oh yes, I've cried over the death of a beloved
> pet or the death of a young man who died at the
> age of 28 of open heart surgery, my client. But
> not until the last few months have I really begun
> to understand the stages of dying as I heard you
> enumerate them today.
>
> In July after several weeks of testing in the
> hospital, they tried to determine why I lost sen-
> sation and function of my legs and the vision

in one eye. I was informed only after demanding to know that I had multiple sclerosis. My neurologist told my husband to "let her think that it is neuritis."

I had just finished teaching a college course in the Rehabilitation Counseling Program on the Medical Aspects of Disabilities. I knew I had to have something serious after having had a brain scan, an EEG, orbital x-rays, an electromyogram and a spinal tap. My own diagnostic considerations were a brain tumor, spinal cancer or multiple sclerosis. Finally I coerced my husband to tell me after I could perceive in his looks that he knew.

I cried, denied, was angry, resentful, "why me?"—the whole thing. I kept seeing the severely ill, afflicted MS wheelchair patients I had worked with as a student, who were dying or dead by my standards.

I was just 33 with a neat husband whom I loved very much, an 8-year-old son, a lovely home I had just begun to feel deserving to live in. I had received my degree in rehabilitation counseling and was working in a hospital with lovely people. Then, wham, MS! I was barely able to walk due to weakness and was afraid I would not be able to keep my new and dearly loved job.

My husband, 2 weeks after my discharge from the hospital, said he wanted a divorce, wanted to live somewhere else and alone. He was not willing to help care for my son, so the doctor convinced me that I should place him with a family to keep him in the same school.

Then I lost my home. I could not make the house payments working full-time, but particularly not, if only part-time. I was barely able to drive. And I thought I was slowly going insane because I never would wake up from what seemed like a month-long bad dream. I wanted to die if I was not dying.

I could not run, play tennis, feel sex, read books. What I could do and was doing was not living but going through an excruciatingly difficult existence. I got to the very bottom of my depression and decided to use sleeping pills to go to sleep and never have to feel the pain of further loss and confusion and the hard work of putting together a meaning where none seemed to exist anymore. But I could not do it.

With 3 bottles of sleeping pills sitting on a table in a borrowed beach house, I slowly found (while trying to write a letter of explanation to my boss) that the meaning is *within* you, not outside. It is not quantity but quality that counts. "Yesterday is dead and gone and tomorrow's out of sight. . . ." (as the song states). So we have to live it fully and find what turns us on, because no one else can do that for us.

It finally came back to me that I CARED ABOUT ME! And many of my warm, honest, real friends cared. They came and sat down at my bedside, held my hand when I cried and cried with me. Or when I could not talk, they would call and talk to me. They did not send flowers, cards or letters to "cheer me up."

I just wanted to tell you, Dr. Ross, I guess my story is a different kind of facing death and dying, but it feels very much akin to the experiences you have had with your patients. Also, I am tremendously glad to be alive and I cherish each moment now while quite aware of having my business finished if I should die tomorrow. And I am not afraid of death anymore!

With love and admiration,

Carolyn Strite

PHYSICAL DESTINY

I tried to explain to Carolyn what we had learned about physical destiny. We knew from our life-after-death research that suicide patients, while they are not punished or judged or condemned after death, lose all their positive growth experiences gained during this lifetime. They have to return into a physical body to be reborn again and pass the same tests, except usually more difficult than during the previous existence. This is not a punishment, but grace or a gift from God as another chance. No one is allowed to return to the source, to God, from where we all come, without having earned all the positive experiences that are possible in the physical lifetime.

The sole purpose of the physical existence is to grow and to become in harmony between the physical, emotional, intellectual and spiritual parts, or quadrants, that comprise every human being. We were all created by the same God, from the same Source, and are all given the gifts of perfection in order to achieve all positive experiences in the physical plane in one single lifetime. It is those who have been depriving themselves of the opportunity, the chance to grow through the windstorms of life, those who are dragged down by their own negativity and their pain—most often self-imposed—of grief, shame, fear or guilt, that are not able to complete their mission and their destiny and have to be reincarnated into another physical lifetime.

There are a great many misconceptions regarding rebir
and its purpose. Rebirth is for one purpose and one purpo
only: It is God's gift to us. It is our chance to learn wh
we decide we have yet to learn, it is to grow to perfecti
in order to return "back home."

Accepting the challenge, Carolyn was able to mobili
her own inner resources, her own inner strength. She w
able not only to function as a counselor but to help a gre
many other multiple sclerosis patients because of her ov
life experiences and her own growth work, her own hones
courage and love for her fellow man.

It was several years later that I received a phone call o
evening during which time she said good-bye to me. S
again told me that she had lost her ability to function, th
she was alone, that she missed her child and her marri
life. She said that she was barely able to work and earn
living and that the quality of life was such that she had
terminate it before she "became a vegetable." She also e
plained to me most honestly that she called me a few m
ments prior to taking her own life but had the urge to than
me for what I had done for her. She also wanted to as
one great favor of me, and that was to accept her wi
unconditional love, which explicitly meant to her that
would not notify any next of kin nor would I call the poli
department to rescue her in an attempt to save her life.

I told her that it was her own free choice but that sh
should know that she had an alternative, and that I woul
wait at seven o'clock the following Monday at the chap
in Santa Barbara and hoped that she would sit there an
wait for me. This was three days prior to the worksho
mentioned earlier. I arrived in Santa Barbara the nig
before and was barely able to sleep. In the wee mornin
hours I went out to this incredibly beautiful chapel. It ha
a cross over the altar and a huge window with an unusual

beautiful tree growing behind it, a symbol of the growth and the life that comes through pain and sacrifice. It was because of this symbolic image that I had chosen that place.

At six o'clock I saw a figure coming out of the shadows into the light. It was my friend who had multiple sclerosis who held onto this straw of hope and the higher choice of trying to give herself another chance. She became the truest gift to this workshop and has since not only survived but has improved her health so much that she is, years later, working full time and raising her son, who finally joined her. She has touched more lives of more patients as well as healthy people than I could have imagined.

It is experiences like this that happen around the workshops—before, in between and afterward—that keep us going and give us strength, courage and conviction that we are on the right path.

Another of the moving experiences that we have observed during these five very intensive days of sharing is something that repeats itself in almost every workshop. That is the gift of cancer patients who have been on chemotherapy and have lost all their hair. They appear usually with a scarf or a very good wig on their head, and compensate with makeup and a lot of attention to their physical appearance. It is in the middle of the workshop usually that they finally share with the group their own frustration with their own self-image, their shame that somebody could touch them and hug them and their wig would fall off. In almost every workshop toward the end, they all, without prompting, move toward this shame and fear by lifting their wigs up and presenting themselves to the whole group, bald as they were when they were born.

The tears and the relief of this type of sharing is enormous. Another similar experience happened with a woman who had had a colostomy and was so ashamed of her body that she had covered all the mirrors in her house for the past fifteen years. When she finally shared this embarrassment with the group, we asked her to show the colostomy to every single member of the workshop participants. She did this very reluctantly, and very much full of shame and fear and resistance. The result of it was that she went home and removed the covers from the mirrors. She looks at least ten years younger now and is no longer carrying shame, guilt and rejection about her own imperfect body.

LETTING GO

There are some very special moments in some of our workshops which all by themselves would be most insignificant. Yet in the context of where the group is at the given time, they become most significant. At one point we were just discussing the issue of letting go and the whole philosophy of the meaning and purpose of suffering, of losses and of death. We talked about the possibility of growth and new life coming from a death experience—new life in the sense of a new awareness, a new sensitivity, a different kind of compassion and understanding for our fellow man. Suddenly a bird hit the window in our conference room.

We took a brief break, trying to help the bird, making him comfortable, seeing if there was anything that we were able to do for him. He was obviously quite numb and injured and we had no idea whether he would survive. While holding him in such a way that it would not frighten or hurt him, I watched as he put his little head to the side and died in my hands. It was a brief intermezzo during one of our breaks, but one that led someone to remember the saying:

> If I can stop one heart from breaking, I shall not live in vain; if I can ease one life from aching, or cool one pain, or help one fainting robin into his nest again, I shall not live in vain.

We decided to bury the bird under a tree, and the ritual of the burial of the bird touched upon many memories. Some were happy, loving memories of parents who were willing to make a funeral for a pet for their children's sake. Others recalled losing a pet and having it replaced by over-anxious parents who went to the pet shop before the child returned from school. Naturally this disguise is soon discovered because of the different behavior of the animal, and the child's trust level decreases rapidly.

So this little dying bird in our hand, and the funeral under the tree on the last evening, served in a sense the same purpose as those who were willing to share. It touched the pool of repressed pain.

It is small incidents like this that made the parents at the workshop aware of how important it is to even share the little deaths with their children, since the death of a pet can be as painful to a youngster who has chosen an animal as his favorite love object as the death of a child is to a parent.

15

Spiritual Awareness and Evolution

AFTER THE FIRST DAY of intellectual sharing an
introductions and two days of emotional experiences, th
group begins to feel an incredible upsurge of feelings c
love, compassion and understanding—never experienced o
felt before.

A convicted, just released murderer was invited by severa
women to spend some time at their homes with their familie
in order to help him with adjustment issues in the outsid
world. He responded with awe and disbelief by saying
"Hey! Didn't you hear I killed my father?" Oh, yes, the
did hear. But they also heard his previous story of chil
abuse, of constant sadistic torture of his siblings, of constan
sexual abuse of his sisters, of the pleading, desperate an
frightened mother who was unable to receive help from
social agencies and unable to protect her children. Yes, they
heard the fact that a judge found him guilty of homicide
that he spent the best years of his life in jail and that n
one seemed to remember the teachings of Christ and th
lessons on understanding and forgiveness. Yes, they wer
willing and happy to take him home. . . .

An elderly nun who was raised with guilt and fear o
condemnation had the courage to express her deep sense o
unfairness and rage over her treatment by a mother superio
and preceded her work with an earnest prayer to Jesus t

allow her to curse and express her feelings in order to serve better and get rid of her accumulated bitterness and negativity. Her prayer at the end was so indescribably moving that six other nuns and two priests immediately followed by openly and honestly sharing their own unfinished business, which included incest, homosexuality, misuse of confession and physical longings forbidden to those who dedicate their lives to these professions.

This is the time when externalization is completed and a sense of great gratitude overwhelms the group as a whole. It is an appreciation for the gifts of sharing and honesty, which functions as a catalyst, a trigger that gets others in touch with long-repressed unfinished business. And as each only shares perhaps one single story of their lives, they touch 8o others, and thus the ripple effect begins to show.

On Thursday morning, after our usual singing and silence (copied from the Quaker meetings), I start my sharing of my own evolution, much of which is described in Gill's biography of my life. I share how I was raised as a triplet, devoid of an individual identity, and use this as an example of grace and blessing as it helped me to understand others with similar problems. We talk about our physical and spiritual destiny, about men's free choice. We share with the group the letter of a nine-year-old child, Dougy, in which he asked, "What is life, what is death and why do little children have to die?" We shared my answer to him, which is now available as the "Dougy Letter" through Shanti Nilaya and which has reached thousands of people all over the world.

We share what we have personally experienced through the sharing of those who were near death, of little ones' communication and awareness of their loved ones just prior to their deaths, and naturally I tell them about my own incomprehensible yet life-changing mystical experiences.

We complete Thursday by listing all the universal laws,

congruent with Christ's teachings and contained in the teach
ings of all great religions: Muslims, Christians, Jews, Hin
dus, Sufis and others. They can then begin to evaluate th
events of their own lives, begin to understand the so-calle
coincidences which we call divine manipulations; and the
become more open to and aware of our own control of ou
destiny by taking personal responsibility for all our choice
deeds, words and thoughts!

At the end of our life, the value of it is a direct result o
all the choices we have taken; help comes only when w
have depleted all our resources.

We're all children of one God. We're all here to lear
to grow and to fulfill our destiny, and when we have learne
our lessons we are allowed to graduate. We have to lear
to understand rather than to judge, to give and receive, t
love without expectations and to practice what is so beau
tifully said in Gibran's *Work Is Love Made Visible*.

IRA

Dear Elisabeth,

I am writing this letter concerning my experiences during and subsequent to the Life, Death
and Transitions Workshop which I attended in
April 1978.

Approximately two years prior to the workshop, I began to believe in G-d,* after having
been an agnostic for as long as I can remember.
(This belief stemmed from a "mystical" experience involving the funeral of a very dear aunt.) I
truly felt that I wanted to believe, but needed

* Orthodox Jews do not spell out the word of God in Hebrev
or any other language.

"proof." Despite this newfound belief, I didn't do anything differently with my life, except read much philosophy and books about death and dying, including your books.

The workshop, for me, was a very moving experience. Participation in the workshop gave me as a physician the opportunity to share in a very real way the traumas that so many people had gone through and survived. Indeed, not only had they survived, but had grown from these "windstorms" in their lives. What the workshop proved was that this growth could occur if we don't get caught up in negative emotions like guilt, fear and anger.

The feeling I got during those five days was extremely high both emotionally and spiritually, which I find almost impossible to express in words.

Your sharing about your contacts with Spirit Guides at the conclusion of the workshop somehow made a deep impression upon me. I presume that up to that point, I couldn't imagine how G-d could know our every thought and action. The intermediary of Guides (Guardian Angels) seemed right to me on a gut level, and made the necessary connection for me to deepen my faith.

Subsequent to the workshop, I have found that I am much more *alive* than I have ever been, and look forward to life's *windstorms* as challenges, and not as disruptions and events to fear and worry about. Also, since then, I have gotten more involved with my religion, Judaism, and am now an observant (Orthodox) Jew. I am now deeply involved in Chassidic Judaism, which I have found to be very compatible with your teachings regarding life after life, Guardian Angels and an

All-Knowing and All-Loving (nonjudgmentally) Supreme Being, who provides us with no more than we can handle (and always in the best interest of our soul's growth). We also believe as you have taught, that there are no coincidences or accidents in life and that everything that we encounter is meant for us to learn from, and that a principal purpose in life is to serve G-d by helping our fellow human beings to ease their suffering. Certainly, you and your workshops do just that!

I hope this letter is helpful to you, and please feel free to use all, or part of it for any purpose you deem worthy.

With all my love and best wishes for continued success in the work you are doing to improve mankind's lot on this planet.

Sincerely yours,
Ira

TOM

Dear Elisabeth,

Approximately one year ago I attended the five-day "Life, Death, and Transition" workshop in Oceanside, California. I regard that event as a major turning point in my life, on both an intellectual and a spiritual level. Let me share with you some of my feelings concerning externalization of repressed negative feelings.

As a member of a family raised in large part on the belief that men in our society need to be "strong," to repress negative feelings of dislike, anger, and depression, I found that, although externally I appeared calm and tranquil, I very occasionally would erupt in an almost insane anger. At times, this tended to endanger myself or others. For the two years prior to the workshop, this occasional eruption of violent anger was endangering my marriage and I was in the depths of a totally debilitating depression. The workshop made me realize that everyone feels anger, hate, sadness and revenge at times, that this was not unhealthy, and that there are satisfying, acceptable ways of releasing those negative feelings. However, even more importantly, I learned to experience close, nonjudgmental love among a large group of friends, a love unfettered by jealousy, guilt, bias, or regret.

The past year has been an exercise in growth and learning about myself and my reactions to other people. I have learned to externalize my feelings, both positive and negative, rather than to keep them bottled in, and in so doing found that life may not always be beautiful but it is worth experiencing to its fullest.

I am a physician and not an expert in law or criminology, but I am convinced that everyone could benefit from learning what I have learned through the "Life, Death, and Transition" workshop. I believe this to be especially true with people who tend to internalize negative feelings, which explode in crimes of violence and pain. This occurs because those internalized, repressed feelings are suddenly all projected onto one object or person, usually after only a small, or even imagined, provoking incident. I believe the workshop could help prevent this type of build-up.

Love to you all.

Tom

CHUCK AND FRAN

Dear Elisabeth:

The Growth and Transition workshop that I attended a year and a half ago was certainly a turning point in my life. Prior to that workshop, I had a significant amount of trouble in relationships, especially with my anger, and a moderate amount of difficulty with grief. I certainly suffered with anxieties as well and have found that the techniques you taught at the workshop do work, without question.

For approximately one year, I worked very hard on externalizing my anger, and my grief, when the opportunity arose. I have found that my personality has changed remarkably and my contemporaries can certainly verify this. This change has definitely been for the better. Although I do not feel a continuous total sense of peace, I have certainly had many more peak experiences than in the past and feel very optimistic in my continued emotional growth.

This has had a great ramification in my practice, of course, and at home as well. Franny, my wife, also attended a workshop and feels that the workshop was a turning point for her as well. She has been able to resolve many of her latent hostile feelings.

Our follow-up has been mostly with the Course

in Miracles and we have found this to be an excellent form of spiritual psychotherapy. To say "excellent" is to put it mildly of course.

I have had the opportunity to work with a number of inmates at the Washington State Penitentiary and although I have not counseled them emotionally, I am certain that these techniques would be very beneficial for these inmates, as I have found they are very fearful as well as angry. Not only would the inmates benefit from this but the guards would as well. There is a cycle that goes on in the local penitentiary that must be broken. The technique taught at the workshop is practical and easy to implement, provided the person is willing. I have encouraged a number of people to utilize this technique. About one-third of those I have talked to do utilize it and there is, without question, a great improvement in their lives and relationships.

Please feel free to use our names and to reprint this letter in any way that you feel appropriate. We extend our best wishes to all of you at Shanti Nilaya for a wonderful holiday season.

Love,
Chuck and Fran

BERNIE

In December 1979 I attended an Elisabeth Kübler-Ross Workshop on life, death and transition. At that time, I experienced very significant changes in myself and saw them happen in the entire group of participants. I believe that the techniques utilized allow us to heal ourselves and free ourselves of the problems of the past in a safe and constructive manner. An element of spirituality is obviously present which I believe is an enormous help to the sick and underprivileged in dealing with their daily problems.

The ability to change oneself and control oneself is obviously an important end result, but more importantly, this is an ongoing change that does not stop with the experience itself, but is one upon which the individual can build. The victim role can be given up.

I believe it is this type of work that is extremely important and would heartily recommend support of this project. We know that mental health creates the appropriate setting for continued physical health and obviously both relate to one's role in society. The place to start is with this type of program, and making it available, as I hope you will do, will create results that we can all be proud of and hopefully project to a larger number of people.

Dr. Ross, because of her unique skills and experience, is the ideal person to initiate this type of program. Her background and her long experience in this area will certainly produce positive change and results. If we can create a small ripple, perhaps it will spread and grow into a wave that will make significant inroads on the problems of our society.

If I sound somewhat grandiose, forgive me, but I have seen what this can do in my personal life, the lives of my friends, and patients.

I know that it is the way to proceed.

Bernie

16
Evaluating the Outcome

❧❧

VERY OFTEN WE ARE ASKED about the results of our workshops. Of course, emotional changes and emotional healings are difficult to quantify. Above all, there is the matter of privacy where our workshop participants are concerned. I have always insisted on absolute confidentiality in the Life, Death and Transition Workshops. Yet there have been so many people interested in our work in terms of its outcomes that the pressure to examine this question statistically led us to see if there were not a way we could do this with sensitivity.

As it happens in many workshops, the participants feel good immediately after the attendance at such a sharing week, only to have a let-down after returning home. We wanted to be sure that this was not the case with our people. We also needed to be sure that their benefits were not just temporary "highs" but the beginning of a continuous growth process.

Just as we began seriously looking at this question, a way to accomplish what we sought to accomplish was given to us. Col. John B. Alexander, a U.S. Army officer stationed in Washington, D.C., had participated in one of our workshops and contacted us some time later to let us know of his interest in quantifying the results with which he was so impressed during his own experience. Col. Alexander developed what he called the Spirituality Change Survey as part of his dissertation leading to a doctorate in Education from Walden University. The instrument also measured attitudinal changes regarding death, life, self, others, basic values and our workshop itself.

Privacy would be absolutely guaranteed, Col. Alexander assured us, and the data could be gathered by the simple voluntary filling out of a pre-workshop and post-workshop questionnaire. Naturally, we looked at the questionnaire and examined closely the statistical basis of the survey process John had developed. Eventually, the survey instrument went through the critical validation process. I agreed to direct the study and sit at the head of the dissertation committee, and so the survey was undertaken.

We could give you our impressions of the results, but those, of course, would be subjective. So we asked John for permission to quote instead directly from the paper he wrote on the survey results after the data were compiled, and again John gave us the loving gift of his permission to do so in this book. Here are some excerpts:

> The measurement was conducted in two modes. Participants of two workshops, December 1978 and January 1979, were requested to complete pre- and post-workshop instruments. This group we called Group A. A second group, Group B, was also selected from attendance rosters of other workshops conducted between June 1977 and October 1978. They were chosen at random from these rosters. Group A participants were asked to fill out pre- and post-workshop questionnaires at the workshop sites. Group B was contacted by mail and filled out post-tests several months after their workshop experience. This gave us an opportunity to compare immediate results from Group A with long-range results in the second grouping.

Analysis of data revealed that significant changes in spirituality did occur in both Group A and Group B. The cumulative figures for Group A showed 465 of 564 responses, or 82%, indicating positive changes. Group B reflected similar results, with 857 of 1,049 responses, or again, 82%, being judged as indicating positive change. (A total of 87 people provided the total questionnaire responses in Group A, with 244 people surveyed and producing the total responses for Group B.)

A positive shift in the group mean was recorded for every survey item in both groups based on an eleven point scale. It was noted that Group B, the respondents to the mailed survey, reflected significantly higher change on all items. This meant that positive changes were even more pronounced in the group surveyed long after the workshops than in the group surveyed immediately after the sessions concluded.

To further test the reliability of the data gathered, a number of respondents from both groups were telephoned after the questionnaire data were compiled. The results of this telephone survey confirmed the statistical data. Subjectively, it was determined that the telephone respondents indicated an even higher magnitude of positive change than they recorded on the survey instrument.

While positive change in spirituality was reported in all groups, care must be taken in the evaluation of these data. While it does indicate group trends, it cannot become predictive of an individual's response.

John's survey contained not only "check off" type questions, but some open-ended questions to which participants could respond in their own words as well. Here from John's paper are some comparisons of pre-workshop and post-workshop attitudes of participants on death and life:

> Death:
> PRE: "end, termination, sorrow, emptiness"
> POST: "peaceful, absence of fear"
> PRE: "fear, the end, terrifying, pain"
> POST: "moving on, it's o.k."
> PRE: "an escape from life"
> POST: "part of a continuum, a transition"
>
> Life:
> PRE: "existence within a physical case"
> POST: "living each day to the fullest, sharing and giving to one's fellow man"
> PRE: "a very painful, traumatic experience"
> POST: "becoming one with the universe"
> PRE: "essentially a 'physical life'"
> POST: "more like 'spiritual existence/flow of energy'"

John's survey also uncovered dramatic changes in attitudes about self, others, values and the specific subject of spirituality. Some of the comments, again from John's paper:

> Self:
> "Self-doubt, self-pain, self-hate are weights that have been taken off."
> "I love myself more."
> "More accepting of my faults."
>
> Others:
> "More accepting, less judgmental."
> "I can forgive wrongs easier."
>
> Values:
> "I definitely feel closer to God and my friends."
> "Major changes are taking place; achievement ori-

entation replaced by recognition of growth."
"I am more open and sure of my value system."

Spirituality:
"It is the most important thing in my day."
"Experientially I know God's presence."
"I feel more inner contact now."

Finally, being a thorough man, John included in his paper some comments from those participating in the post-data-analysis telephone survey. We'll share a few of these, too. To us they contain no surprises. We have heard these comments often from our workshop participants. The fact that the telephone survey produced such comments independent of us merely confirms the honesty of the remarks made directly to us.

"I know now the connection between mind and spirit."
"I found God at the workshop—I had given up on religion despite a strict upbringing."
"It was the biggest revelation of my life . . . like a metamorphosis."
"It extended my own limits to accept people as they are."

Of course, not every single response to every single question was positive. But John reports that not one of the survey respondents answered all questions negatively. Even our harshest critics had something nice to say about us.

We did not need the survey to prove to us that the workshops brought benefit and growth to people. But even we had to admit surprise when John's survey showed positive and lasting change in 82% of the participants!

This survey is naturally available to anyone who has a serious interest in it. But I want to end this chapter by saying that we are really out to prove nothing. We are not on a crusade for people's minds, and it is of no importance, really, if a great many people do not accept our methods or share our beliefs.

My life has been spent on a search for the truth, as well as avenues to share everything I have learned with people in ways that will be lovingly helpful. I believe that anything done with the intention of helping others will, in the end, always work out. Even mistakes made with honesty and purity can produce positive outcomes. So we are not nearly so concerned with ways we can impress people with the results of past workshops as we are with developing ways we can reach even more people with the teachings we have been given by those who have shared with us in these sessions. As I have said so often, they have been our teachers. What we do is share their lessons, and the beautiful gifts they bring us.

17
Epilogue

꒦꒷

I HAVE INCLUDED these few letters here, chosen virtually at random from the many thousands we have received (and continue to receive daily) because they tell better than I ever could what these workshops have meant to those who attend.

Many of those who register for the workshop (particularly those in the helping professions—the doctors, the nurses, the priests and ministers, the social workers and therapists) expect to be exposed to a week of didactic programs and lectures, with perhaps a question-and-answer session here and there and maybe a chance for a little sharing of experiences. They come armed with tape recorders and notebooks and pencils.

And when the workshop is over many of these participants come to us and say, "This isn't at all what I expected." Then, to a person, they tell us that the workshop was much more meaningful, much more valuable, much more to the point in an experiential way, than anything we could have told them in a series of standup presentations with podium and blackboard.

We have always pointed out to those who minister to the sick and to the dying that they must learn to step *away* from their professional roles, and reach out instead as human beings. But to reach out as human beings, we must be "together," or "whole," or whatever words you want to put to it. I am saying that we must have finished as much of our own unfinished business as possible. We must have come to grips with the many deaths—the "little" deaths we encounter every day, and the big deaths that mark important passages in our lives—that have marked the landscape of our own particular journey, or we can never truly help another person fully. The reason is simple. The work will be too threatening. Too many of one's own buttons will be pushed if these intensely personal issues have not been resolved. It is not at all surprising to me that the suicide rate among psychiatrists is higher than for any other group of people. These are people who are making an honest and a very real attempt to heal others, yet have not really healed themselves.

So, yes, we do startle a few of the participants at the beginning of the real "work" sessions, when they see the tools we bring out—the mattress and the rubber hose and the old telephone books to be shredded to pieces. And they are taken aback sometimes when the work begins, and when one person after another moves spontaneously to the front of the room and begins banging away at the mattress with the hose, or completely demolishing the Yellow Pages as they release their pent-up rage and guilt, fear and pain. Finally these people had a safe environment to cry out in pain, to spit out their anger, to curse themselves or the gods or whomever they felt deserved it. And in thus crying out the emotion, they released themselves from being its captive.

Those who become startled—who came expecting a nice, tidy little professional seminar on how to handle the problems of death and dying—soon find their own emotions stirring . . . just as they would were they in an emergency room or in an intensive-care unit and found themselves exposed to, and touched by, the pain and grief and turmoil of others.

And in our setting they can take off the mask and admit that they, too, have these pains and fears and guilts and angers. And they can at last begin to let go. And then they no longer have to insulate themselves from those in pain.

But the workshop is more than just a process of externalization and expulsion of negative emotions. The larger message is the same as the lesson we have learned from personal work with so many dying patients. It is the message of how to live, as well as how to die, or how to help others die. Only when you are not afraid to live will you be unafraid to die. Only when you have lived *your* life fully can you begin to help others do the same, and thus face the moment of *their* death.

Is it ever too early or too late to attend one of these workshops? The answer is basically no, although there are, naturally, exceptions. A middle-aged couple arrived together one day in order to deal with the death of their son. The father especially had a tremendous amount of repressed rage and anger at the world, at God, at the helping professions. He seemed stunned and unwilling to mingle with others and became quite resentful when others shared their pain —especially other bereaved parents. He was unable to listen to others in pain and felt truly that his tragedy was greater than any other.

Although his wife was ready to get involved, he pulled her out of the group and left on Tuesday without notice. A few weeks later he sent us a letter through a lawyer, suing for not offering what he expected! Needless to say, a few letters from other bereaved parents who were more than helped made them retreat.

Another lady in her eighties arrived even less prepared for what she was going to experience. She had been given the workshop as a Christmas gift by her son, a physician, and her daughter-in-law, both of whom had previously attended. She sat stiffly and perhaps stunned for the first day

until quite late at night. She never said much but looke
in amazement over the group of seventy-five people, mc
of them seated on the floor. She never took her eyes fro
the person who shared and only once casually remarke
that she had never seen such a potpourri of people, sk
colors, ages, races, religious and economic backgrounds
one room.

She smoked one cigarette after another and never ev
missed a session. Since she was our oldest participant an
one of the few who sat in a chair, right next to me, I ende
up lighting at least a hundred cigarettes for her daily, an
in appreciation for her unusual tenacity, I rewarded he
with my leather-pouch lighter when she left. She was ve
touched by the deep friendships that developed in such
short time and made her rounds hugging and kissing every
one good-bye.

Although we greatly discourage reunions and fan club
we did have a reunion, unexpected and unplanned by m
two weeks later. I happened to return to Hawaii for a on
hour lecture and thus had to stay overnight in Honolulu t
catch a plane the next morning for Chicago. Many forme
workshop participants greeted me at the end of the presen
tation and asked me to join them for a pot-luck dinne
Little did I know that our old lady had "plotted" this re
union and organized an incredibly beautiful dinner in
private home with everyone bringing their favorite dish
flowers, leis and a display of food fit for a king. They ha
flown in all the workshop participants from all the island
including patients on stretchers, quadriplegics and whee
chair patients. It looked like a feast held at Lourdes.

When everybody was greeted, our friend walked in, beau
tifully dressed, looking twenty years younger in a whit
pajama suit with red poppy flowers and a big happy smil
on her face. Again she made her rounds, hugging everyone
then stopped in front of me and with an almost mischievou

grin lit a cigarette for me! In a brief speech she stated that she had learned her last lesson, she had learned to make friends with people from every race, every conceivable background. She needed this reunion as a reality testing to know if our mutual love and understanding would last. She wanted to know if those same people would still hug her when the workshop was over!

With satisfied contentment she finished her last cigarette, turned slowly around and bid us to the table. Her last remarks were: "I have learned my last lesson, let us eat together, my physical body is getting very tired. . . ." As she approached the table, she collapsed. We carried her into the master bedroom and sang all her favorite songs to her: "I'll be loving you always," "Kumbaya," holding her, loving her. When the paramedics arrived to take her to Kaiser Hospital, they were so overwhelmed by the atmosphere of peace and acceptance that they joined in the singing as they carried her out to the ambulance.

She died a few moments later, never regaining consciousness. What an appropriate death for a gallant lady, who originally only came "because I am not supposed to waste such an expensive Christmas present"!

She died surrounded by love, care and her beloved music.

It has to be said that in this book we emphasized the growth work, the individual sharing during these five days. I have said very little about the content of the last day, when the group feels a sense of uncommon togetherness after having shared so much pain and released so much anguish.

It is at that time that the group begins to settle down in a calm and open manner, reflecting on the reasons why man makes life so miserable for him/herself when it was designed to be so simple and so full of miracles. We usually spend the last day together sharing some of our research in life and life after death, including some of my mystical experiences and the ways that men can know (rather than believe)

about our physical-spiritual evolution, about our existenc
beyond this physical life and—most important—about th
lessons we have to learn, especially the practice of uncon
ditional love for all of mankind, others as well as ourselves

I am grateful to those whose letters have appeared in thi
book, because through their eyes, not my own, you hav
been able to see and hear and feel what this lesson has mean
to them.

I am grateful, too, to all the thousands who have attended
the Life, Death and Transition Workshops all over th
world, because each of them has been our teacher, bringin;
a wonderful gift to our groups as a whole, and to each o
us individually. And we know from their postworksho;
reactions, letters and telephone calls that they also took :
gift *with* them—proving another of the universal laws: Al
true benefits are mutual.

A friend and colleague of mine, Jerry Jampolsky, entitle
one of his most popular books *Love Is Letting Go of Fear*
We have tried to put this book about our workshops togethe
for those who are searching for a way to accomplish thi
goal. As we have stated so many times in lectures an
writings, in our workshops and in our encounters witl
patients all over the world: fear and guilt are the only
enemies of man. We create our own heaven and our own
hell right here on earth. Life was created to be very simple
and beautiful, but most of us turn it into an ungratifying
"making a living but never really learning how to live.'
Why does it take a diagnosis of a terminal illness before a
person reevaluates his life and priorities? Why do we postpone the things we want most out of life? Why do we spend
most of our lives gratifying someone else's expectations and
never our own? Why do we not appreciate life at its fullest
and celebrate every moment of the many miracles that are
around and within us?

The participants of these workshops begin to see some

of the answers to these questions. In their own labor, their own struggles shared, they give a gift to themselves and those they share it with. My favorite, Kahlil Gibran (in *The Prophet*), summarizes perhaps in the most poetic manner what can be learned by those who have the courage to review their lives, their attitudes and those behaviors that may prevent them from living fully:

> . . . But I say to you that when you work, you fulfill a part of earth's furthest dream, assigned to you when that dream was born,
>
> And in keeping yourself with labour you are in truth loving life . . .
>
> You have been told that life is darkness, and in your weariness you echo what was said by the weary.
>
> And I say that life is indeed darkness save when there is urge,
>
> and all urge is blind save when there is knowledge,
>
> and all knowledge is vain save when there is work,
>
> and all work is empty save when there is love;
>
> And when you work with love you bind yourself to yourself, and to one another, and to God.
>
> And what is it to work with love?
>
> It is to weave the cloth with threads drawn from your heart, even as if your beloved were to wear that cloth.
>
> It is to build a house with affection, even as if your beloved were to dwell in that house.
>
> It is to sow seeds with tenderness and to reap the harvest with joy, even as if your beloved were to eat the fruit.
>
> It is to charge all things you fashion with a

breath of your own spirit, and to know that all the blessed dead are standing about you and watching.

Thank you for allowing me to share an important pa of my life with you. I am blessed by your existence.

ELISABETH K. ROSS, M.D.

Index

ABOUT THE AUTHORS

Elisabeth Kübler-Ross is a medical doctor, psychiatrist, and internationally renowned thanatologist. Her other books, known to millions of readers, include *On Death and Dying* (1969), *Questions and Answers on Death and Dying* (1974), *Living with Death and Dying* (1981), and *On Children and Death* (1983), all of which are available from Touchstone Books. She lives in Headwaters, Virginia.

Mal Warshaw, a writer and professional photographer, has published four other books, including *To Live Until We Say Good-bye* (1978) with Elisabeth Kübler-Ross. He lives and works in Westport, Connecticut.

Other books from ELISABETH KÜBLER-ROSS

Available at your local bookstore or from Macmillan Publishing Company. To order, please fill out the order form below and mail to: Macmillan Publishing Company, Special Sales Department, 866 Third Avenue, New York, NY 10022.

Line Sequence	Quantity	ISBN	Title	Price	Total
1	_____	0020864906	LIVING WITH DEATH AND DYING, pb	$ 5.95	_____
2	_____	0025671103	ON CHILDREN AND DEATH, cl	$12.95	_____
3	_____	002076670X	ON CHILDREN AND DEATH, pb	$ 4.95	_____
4	_____	0026050609	ON DEATH AND DYING, cl	$14.95	_____
5	_____	0020891304	ON DEATH AND DYING, pb	$ 4.95	_____
6	_____	0020891504	QUESTIONS AND ANSWERS ON DEATH AND DYING, pb	$ 4.95	_____
7	_____	0020220006	WORKING IT THROUGH, pb	$ 5.95	_____

Sub-total _____

Please add postage and handling costs—$1.00 for the first book and 50¢ for each additional book _____

Sales tax—if applicable _____

TOTAL _____

_____ Enclosed is my check/money order payable to Macmillan Publishing Company.

_____ Bill my _____ MasterCard _____ Visa Card # _____

Expiration date _____ Signature _____

Charge orders valid only with signature

Control No. [   ]   Ord. Type [REG]

For charge orders only:

Bill to: _____

Ship to: _____

_____ Zip Code _____

Lines Units
[   ] [   ]

Bill to: _____

_____ Zip Code _____

For information regarding bulk purchases, please write to Special Sales Director at the above address. Publisher's prices are subject to change without notice. Allow 3 weeks for delivery.

FC #278